THE SOCIAL HISTORY OF EDUCATION

GENERAL EDITOR : VICTOR E. NEUBURG

Second Series — No. 1

OF THE

EDUCATION OF THE POOR

OF THE

EDUCATION OF THE POOR

BEING THE FIRST PART OF

A DIGEST

OF THE

Reports of the Society for Bettering
the Condition of the Poor

REPRINTS OF ECONOMIC CLASSICS

AUGUSTUS M. KELLEY · PUBLISHERS
NEW YORK 1971

Published by

WOBURN BOOKS LIMITED

9 RUSSELL CHAMBERS, BURY PLACE, LONDON WC1

First edition   1809
New impression   1970

SBN 7130 0010 4

Published in the U. S. A. by

AUGUSTUS M. KELLEY, PUBLISHERS

Clifton, New Jersey

Printed in Great Britain by Clarke, Doble & Brendon Ltd.
Plymouth and London

OF THE

EDUCATION OF THE POOR;

BEING THE FIRST PART OF

A DIGEST

OF THE

REPORTS OF THE SOCIETY FOR BETTERING
THE CONDITION OF THE POOR:

AND CONTAINING

A SELECTION OF THOSE ARTICLES

WHICH HAVE

A REFERENCE TO EDUCATION.

Hoc opus, hoc studium parvi properamus et ampli,
Si Patriæ volumus, si nobis vivere cari.   Hor.

LONDON:

PRINTED FOR THE SOCIETY,
BY W. BULMER AND CO. CLEVELAND-ROW;
AND SOLD BY J. HATCHARD, PICCADILLY, AND THE REST OF
THE BOOKSELLERS TO THE SOCIETY.

1809.

[*The following Work is entirely selected from the Reports of the Society, with exception of the Preface, and of the Articles No. 8, 14, 24, 25, and 28 The last Paper (No. 28) is written with a view of giving an example of the facility, with which some of the suggestions in the Reports might be adopted in the habitations of the Poor. Copies of the last Paper, as a separate publication, are added with a view to Distribution, if the Subscribers should approve it.*]

CONTENTS.

PREFACE.

THE CARE AND INSTRUCTION OF THE POOR form the peculiar and beautiful characteristic of the Christian Religion. The giving of light to those who walked in darkness, and the rescuing of the great mass of mankind from the error of Pagan Idolatry, is the favourite subject of the great evangelical prophet;* who refers with joy to that *intellectual period* of the Christian Church, when " all her " children should be taught of the Lord,"— when " the light should break upon her as " the morning,"—and " the Gentiles should " come to her light, and Kings to the " brightness of her rising."

* Isaiah.

THE same benevolent duty has been prescribed and exemplified by the DIVINE FOUNDER of our religion, " who was given " to be a light to the Gentiles." His Apostles enforced, and the primitive Christians practised, what their blessed master had enjoined; until the predicted period of Papal and Mahommedan superstition and tyranny involved, at the same time, the eastern and western hemisphere, in ignorance, vice, and slavery. It was then the prevalent sentiment,—and ROME and MECCA held the same creed,—that the general dissemination of knowledge was *a dangerous thing ;* for the multitude never listened so credulously to imposture, or submitted * so willingly to

* DR. FERRIAR has referred to a curious instance of coincidence upon this subject.—BRANTOME observes, that the principles of the reformed religion are adverse to arbitrary power, and gives that as the reason, why " FRANCIS THE FIRST, that *wise prince*, hated the " Reformers, and was a *little hard* with them, ordering " the hereticks of his day to be BURNT ALIVE." Brantome gravely adds, as to Francis's contemporary, *Soliman the Magnificent*, that " THE GREAT SULTAN " WAS OF THE SAME OPINION ;" and gives the sapient Mussulman's speech upon the occasion.

slavery, as when debased by vice, and blinded by ignorance.

THE difference between the most pure and the most corrupt state of christianity, is in nothing

View of the christian world.

so distinguishable, as in this respect;—that while the exertions of the latter are directed to keep the great mass of the people in ignorance, the former is employed in freely and benevolently offering instruction to all.— Happily, the dark period of slavery and superstition is now past. When the light of Reformation arose in Europe, the delusions of Popery vanished away; and the Christian privilege of " being *wise* to salva- " tion" was restored to a considerable part of the civilized world. It is impossible, however, to take a view of Christianity, without lamenting that, even in Protestant countries, only a very small part of our brethren are as yet in the entire possession of Christian instruction. And if we look beyond the pale of our own reformed church, it is most afflicting to humanity to notice the dark and forlorn state, in which millions of Christians, gifted with reason, and heirs of immortality, have been kept for a succession of centuries ; and to contemplate the savage cruelty and disgusting sensuality, which have resulted from the obscurity and blindness to which they have been devoted. Omitting every invidious observation on any part of modern Europe, I refer to ABYSSINIA,* and to some other parts of the East, where the Christian name and profession exist, where theological controversies, zealous bigotry and superstitious observances are extremely prevalent, and at the same time the divine spirit of Christianity, and those moral virtues which are its genuine fruits, are utterly unknown.

I AM aware that there have been many,

* In Mr. Bruce's account of the Customs and Religion of Abyssinia, lib. v. cap. 11 and 12, the reader will see an example of a nation, professing Christianity, detesting heresy, strict in ceremonials, and punctiliously orthodox,—yet living in habits of gross sensuality, savage cruelty, and dark and hopeless ignorance.

and still are *some* pious Objections to gene-
and conscientious Chris- ral education.
tians, who dread the consequences of a general diffusion, even of *elementary knowledge*
among the poor.* The miseries which have
attended the very name of *equality* in a neighbouring kingdom, have excited an alarm as
to every thing which can tend to *equalize*
the powers of man ; and have induced some
excellent and well intentioned individuals to
adopt ideas, as distant from truth and polity,
as the dreams of jacobinism.

IN the concerns of this fleeting world, in
the division of the gewgaws
and indulgences, which are Equality.
so generally the objects of pursuit, there
never was, and there never can be, equality.

* Among the topics frequently urged against the *diffusion of knowledge* among our Christian brethren, none
is more earnestly insisted upon than the danger of en-
gendering *pride*. In order to render others content
with IGNORANCE, the friends of *that lady* are perpetually shewing the danger of instruction, and proving
that the *Cassette verte of Pandora* could not have contained
more evils. If Ignorance, say they, is expelled from

The *many* must be impelled to action, by beholding them the property of a few;—attainable only by the diligence and prudence of the individual, or of his ancestor. But in real good,—in the instruction which prepares for moral improvement,—which developes to man the privileges of the HEIR OF IMMORTALITY, and forms his course to future happiness, by virtuous principles, by prudential habits, and by religious feelings, —no difference exists between man and man. The same GOD is rich to all who call upon him.

IN the ornamental branches of the fine arts,—in painting, sculpture, and music, in literary

Degree of education.

attainments and in professional science, EDUCATION must be as various as the condi-

her seat, the vacancy must be filled up by PRIDE, and the other deadly sins. Thus it is that the *pride* of knowledge is presented as a bugbear, to preclude millions of rational creatures from the benefit of instruction ;—while the daily commerce of the world might convince us, that the *pride of knowledge* is nothing,—absolutely nothing to the PRIDE OF IGNORANCE.

tion, situation, and talent of man. But in the elements of knowledge,—the means, not the objects of attainment,—in the acquisition of the *alphabetical and numerical* language,* now easily and generally disseminated by the art of printing, the poor have as good a right to the instruction which illumines and directs their path through life, as the greatest and most elevated of their fellow subjects. Without waiting to receive the Gospel from others, they have as much right of access to its treasures by education, as they have to be admitted to Christ's church by baptism.

AND make them what they should be,— instructed and enlightened christians,—and they will

Civil Society.

all know, that a free and regulated state of

---

* It his been well observed, that the capability of writing, and the knowledge of the elementary parts of arithmetic, (without which a porter cannot keep the petty cash accounts of his employer) is not likely to render the poor discontented with their lot; but that, on the contrary, it would fill them with hope and happiness; for the man who is acquainted with numbers

society contains the greatest portion of happiness, with the smallest alloy of inconvenience,* that can exist in this world. Every individual cannot provide a store-house against scarcity:—but the rich man can; and when famine threatens, the poor as well as the rich are thereby preserved. All cannot climb the laborious heights of science:—but the rich, or (with their aid) those gifted with extraordinary intellectual powers may surmount the difficulties; and the consequent improvements in manufactures, in commerce, and in all the arts and comforts † of

would learn the advantages of frugality, and become saving ; and he might see, that by pursuing such habits, he would not, through all the circumstances of his life, be doomed to the drudgery of daily labour.—*Fox's Comparative View.*

* I should be very sorry that the title to property and pre-eminence should depend on the degradation or unhappiness of others. If the foundation of the enjoyment and intelligence of a few, is to be laid in the misery and ignorance of the many, the sooner such a fabric is dedestroyed, the better. Let us not, however, entertain an opinion so injurious to civil society. If legitimate in form, and duly administered, the happiness of the whole, —of the lowest as well as the highest link in the chain of society—is thereby equally promoted.

† The accommodation of an European prince, (*says*

life, will promote the happiness of the whole. All cannot conduct the helm of state ; but some may direct our counsels, some may lead our armies, and others guide our fleets, in the path of glory; and preserve their countrymen from the miseries, under which the rest of Europe is now groaning, with unparalleled affliction.

LET us not, however, estimate so meanly of the understanding of the cottager, as to think him incapable of per- Its effects on the ceiving that the same law poor. secures to him and his family the enjoyment of their earnings, and to the rich the possession of their wealth ;—that the same civil sanctions protect the life, the liberty, and the property of the poor, as well as of the opulent; and defend the industrious and honest, from the force and fraud of the

Adam Smith,) does not always so much exceed that of an industrious and frugal peasant, as the accommodation of the latter, exceeds that of many an African king, the absolute master of the lives and liberties of ten thousand naked savages.— *Smith on the Wealth of Nations.*

idle and dissolute.   He will soon know, that with the temperature, the constitution, and the other natural and political advantages of Britain, no region on earth affords such benefits to the general mass of the people, as this happy island.   Favoured in soil, in climate, in religious toleration, in political freedom,—placed in a country where the child of the meanest peasant may look to the highest honours* which he can deserve, —and where equal laws protect him in the possession of whatever industry and talent can earn,—what can he wish, except kindness to himself and EDUCATION for his children ? what, except that Christianity shall be in the hearts, as it is in the mouths, of the other classes of society ?

IN order to make the poor fully comprehend their duties and advantages, let us shew them that we understand our own.—If superiority of

Its demand upon the rich.

* Patere honoris scirent ut cunctis viam,
  Nec generi tribui sed virtuti gloriam.   PHÆDR.

condition is to be respected * as the appointment of GOD, it must be maintained on the
ground of the functions it implies. THE DE-
LIVERY OF THE TALENT IS THE INJUNCTION OF
THE DUTY ; and he, who possesses wealth
and power, occupies a *public station ;* and is
bound to make those possessions the means
of good to others, not the instruments of
avarice, ostentation, or sensuality to himself.

THE establishment of endowed charity
schools, in the beginnning   Endowed charity
of the preceding century,   schools.
does infinite honour to the piety and humanity of that age.   In general however, they
are insufficient ; and, in many instances, the
benefit of the original source of instruction
is diminished, for want of proper channels,
through which the stream of benevolence
should be conducted.   The gross abuses †

* Dr. Paley's Assize Sermon.
† I had once began a list of them. But I found my
number increase so fast, and that *accurate information* as
to the particular facts was so difficult to obtain, that I
discontinued an unpleasing enquiry, which did not

which have existed in *some* of our endowed
schools (as to which you can hardly meet a
new person, or visit a new country, without
hearing of fresh examples) are chiefly confined to the more ancient endowments, and
do not generally apply to those schools,
which have been established since the beginning of Queen Anne's reign.

WITH regard, however, to these latter
Diminution of num- schools, there is another cir-
ber of scholars. cumstance on which I think
it proper to offer some observations, having
in a former instance * only slightly referred
to it. I mean, what the trustees periodically
state in the annual publication of the Society
for promoting Christian knowledge,—that
" *they have thought fit to lessen the number of*
" *children taught in them, that the rest may be*
" *entirely supported ; which is the reason, the*
" *number now taught is short of what it was*
" *formerly.*" How far this is a breach of

appear to promise to be useful in my hands, but to require more potent means of investigation.

* In the introductory Letter to the fourth volume of
the Society's Reports.

trust, I shall not now presume to inquire. Reserving, however, the right of entertaining doubts about the legality, I shall take the liberty of considering its wisdom and policy.

THE usual reason for giving a preference to the suppporting of a *few* scholars, instead of instructing *many*, is, that "the morals of the pupils are corrupted at

Reason given for boarding charity children.

"at home; and that no dependence can be "placed on the conduct of children, while "they have any communication with their "parents."—Weak and imperfect, indeed, must that system of education be, which will not, without contamination, admit of a few hours every day, spent by a child in its parent's cottage. If the short interval between school hours is so suddenly to obliterate all the traces of religious and moral discipline, what is to be the result of the commerce of the world, when they quit the school ? what the present effects of those examples and of that language, with which our streets are disgraced, from the infection of which our charity children, in their hours of play, are not generally protected?

BUT I cannot persuade myself that this is the real objection.—The fact is, that whilst instruction extended to many, confers extensive benefits, a school which *entirely supports* a few, supplies *useful patronage.*—If a servant's child is admitted, the parent can afford to be satisfied with less wages: if that of a needy dependant, our own contribution to our poor friend, becomes less necessary; and if a parish child is the object, the school endowment comes opportunely in aid of the parish rate.

Another reason.

THE proper inquiry is not how convenient patronage may be obtained, but how the most extensive and permanent good can be done. Considering, therefore, the question with this view, I shall observe, in the *first* place, that removing children from their parents for several years, and educating them in a sepa-

Answer to them.

rate establishment, is peculiarly liable to the objections, which have been sometimes (however unjustly) urged against any instruction of the poor, even as day scholars.— It unfits them for a cottage life, and cottage fare. It disqualifies them for hard labour. It raises their views above the condition wherein they were born. It teaches them to undervalue their parents; and breaks and destroys the sacred connection between parent and child, the mutual endearments of which constitute the most valuable blessing of our temporal existence.

2. IT also excludes one of the greatest advantages to be derived from education, in the improvement of the other poor.—The beautiful and affecting narrative, in the Cheap Repository, of the sinful father reformed by the piety of his educated child,* is supported by

Advantage of day scholars.

* See the account of HESTER WILMOT, in the Cheap Repository Tracts.—The reader will also have pleasure in referring to an interesting anecdote given by Mr. RAIKES, of Gloucester. A father of one of

a variety of facts. The examples are numerous. But these effects of pious education
are not confined to individual cases. I have
witnessed in St. Giles's free chapel, many
instances of parents (persons who had not
before thought of a church) attending there
constantly, in consequence of the admission
of their children into the free-school connected with that chapel. And recently, at
Sunderland and Wearmouth, the very opening of the new schools there, brought a
numerous attendance of their parents to
the parish churches.—Again, as to the good
effects produced upon the child's brothers
and sisters, a well disposed boy * of ten or
eleven years of age will teach his younger
friends at home, the first rudiments of know-

his scholars thanked him for the benefit he had himself
received in his School ; being asked how, explained himself thus :—" The good instructions you give my boy,
" he brings home to me ; and IT IS THAT, SIR,
" WHICH HAS MADE ME REFORM MY LIFE."—
Lessons for Young Persons in Humble Life, p. 37.

* I do not mean that sisters are less capable than their
brothers of giving instruction at home. They are com-
monly more acute and intelligent than boys of the same
age.

knowledge, better and more pleasantly than any schoolmaster;—especially if he has been so fortunate as to be taught upon the Madras system, which forms the instructor at a very early age, and makes the power of teaching go hand in hand with the receipt of instruction.

3. CONSIDERED with a view either to difficulty or expense, the comparative effect of teach-

Comparative expense.

ing *day scholars* is almost beyond conception. The cost of maintaining and instructing a boy in one of our charity schools, is from twelve to eighteen guineas a year; that of educating him at a day school,* upon the Reverend Dr. Bell's system, from four to ten shillings a year. I will take their average; that of the former at fifteen guineas a year, that of the latter at seven shillings; and we shall find that the sum of one thousand five hundred guineas, expended

* Mr. LANCASTER, who, in his school in the Borough, has the merit of having carried Dr. BELL's system into execution, upon a very great scale, and with more economy than any other person, has kept the average expense of each boy or girl under four shillings a year.

on the board and tuition of *one hundred children*, would have provided for the *education* of FOUR THOUSAND FIVE HUNDRED day scholars;—and (supposing that among parents, brothers, and sisters, three individuals receive moral benefit from each day-scholar) this trifling sum might have produced moral and religious effects on 18,000 persons.

WHAT then will follow? Do I propose to discontinue the *maintaining* of *any* charity children?—
Suggestions.
By no means. Let them be maintained to the full extent of the founder's intention. But do not deprive the other poor of the portion of general instruction intended for them. Make those endowments subservient to, and not exclusive of, the education of other children. Adopt the system which Dr. Haygarth introduced at Chester * in 1783, and which the Bishop of Durham has recently adopted at Auckland. Admit a

* This account will be found in a subsequent part of this volume. It was originally published in the Society's Reports, vol. ii.

considerable number of day scholars, and make *pre-eminence in the day school,* the motive for admission into the house, as was done with great effect at Chester: or, if the Trust allows it, extend the rule to the day schools of the adjoining district; and, at the same time, abbreviate the term of continuance in the house, so that its benefits may be more extended.—The qualification for admission on the foundation of the Bishop of Durham's school at Auckland, where all the expenses are defrayed by his Lordship, is excellence and regularity in any day school in his diocese. A similar regulation, adopted in other endowments, might supply a stimulus to attention and good conduct, that would be invaluable.

IN the establishment of a general system of education, potent means of action may be derived

Dr. Bell's method.

from the Rev. Dr. BELL's new mode of instruction; which, while it facilitates the attainment of the elements of knowledge, possesses a simplicity and certainty in its operations, that give scope to the exertions of the quickest mind, while they supply energy and activity to the dullest.

THE reader will not easily and correctly appreciate the value of Dr.
Obviates difficulties.
Bell's method, until he has attended to the difficulties, which have been in general considered as impediments to the progress of instruction, and has examined the manner in which Dr. Bell has obviated them. By these means he will trace the operations of an attentive and scientific mind, anticipating and removing difficulties. —I shall state these points separately, and distinctly; in the hope that some, who may not yet be prepared to adopt the whole at once, may however be willing to try the effect in part :—and I shall offer them to the Reader, under the nine following heads.

1. 𝕿𝖍𝖊 𝖎𝖓𝖈𝖆𝖕𝖆𝖈𝖎𝖙𝖞 𝖔𝖋 𝖈𝖔𝖓𝖙𝖎𝖓𝖚𝖊𝖉 𝖆𝖙𝖙𝖊𝖓𝖙𝖎𝖔𝖓 𝖎𝖓 𝖈𝖍𝖎𝖑𝖉𝖗𝖊𝖓.—The imbecility
As to attention.
of young minds makes not only *employment* but even *unvaried amuse-*

ment, in a short time, irksome and unpleasant. Moral writers, in every age, have commented upon this fact. Still, however, in our schools, the attempt is continued, to chain down the attention of youth for two hours and more, to the same object: so that when they come to say their lesson, which requires the fullest exertion of intellect, the powers of application have been already worn out and exhausted.—In Dr. Bell's schools, no lesson is given to a little child, that will occupy more than *five minutes** in the learning. For the saying of it, ten minutes are allowed. The lessons are such as may be acquired easily, and without labour, within the limited time; but the ten minutes which succeed, constitute the period of exertion and improvement. The least want of attention † will then subject a boy, to yield his

---

* What is said here applies to the younger children, in the early period of the instruction. As their habits of attention and application are increased and confirmed, their period for learning their lessons is gradually extended to ten or twelve minutes.

† The call for attention is further increased by the manner in which the lessons are said ; the pupils being

place to a competitor, who is more attentive at the moment. The scholars at this time seem to have acquired new and unknown powers; and will advance more by *saying* one short lesson, than in *learning* two long ones in the usual mode. The consequence is, that children who have with difficulty achieved two tiresome lessons in a morning, will now with eagerness and pleasure, dispatch twelve or fifteen in the same time; while the constant and rapid change of situation and employment, and the renewed contest for places, preclude weariness, excite eagerness, improve intellect, and keep the body in a state of motion and action.

2. **Confused and Imperfect Knowledge.** — In the usual mode, where
Knowledge.
any boy makes a mistake in saying his lesson, the master sets him

arranged round the teacher, and each reading one word of the lesson in his turn, and then (a practice of which nothing but the effects of repeated experiment could justify) each one taking his word backward to the beginning of the lesson again ; and so reading it backwards and forwards, till all the words are thoroughly impressed on the mind.

right. Nothing more, however, passes to produce a permanent effect, or to impress the instruction either on him or on the rest of the class. The time of hearing also is comparatively short, and as soon as it is done, the class proceeds to another lesson. Thus error is frequently blended with instruction, and false and incorrect impressions left in the mind.—In Dr. Bell's schools, if so many as *three mistakes*, however trivial, are made in the course of the hearing, the class is ordered back again to learn and relearn it; and a second lesson is never given them, until they have *all perfectly* learnt the first. But then their progress is not impeded by the dullness or idleness of a single scholar; for if he cannot keep up with the others, he is removed to a lower class, as will be noticed under another head.

3. **The former leſſon being obliterated by the latter.**—This is found
Retention.
to be a common evil, not only in schools, but in the studies of mature life; and we justly estimate the habit of

retaining from what is presented to the mind's eye, all that is valuable, and of rejecting what is not so, as one of the most useful habits that a student can acquire.—The books which Dr. Bell's scholars learn, they go through a second, and sometimes even a third time: and they are not allowed to proceed to another book, until they have completely mastered the former. Their second passage through a book (and still more the third if necessary) is of course more rapid, and does not consume much additional time: but it fixes the whole distinctly and permanently in their minds.

4. **Want of motive to exertion.**—There are in most schools, periods

Exertion.

of examination, when the comparitive diligence and improvement of the pupils are the objects of inquiry, and when their places are fixed accordingly. These examinations, however, are infrequent, and the decisions are not by fixed and unvaried rules.—In the new system, the examination is subject to certain public and known rules, and the relative competition takes place *upon every lesson.* Ten minutes in every quarter of an hour, or at least in every twenty minutes, are thus occupied in this contest for pre-eminence ; and the more diligent scholar claims his precedence, not from the master, but under the established and promulgated laws of the school. The taking of places on these occasions is instantaneous. The boy who has failed, resigns his rank to his class-mate, without waiting for any decision on a claim, the justice whereof they all feel. Attention is thus kept up, and a spirit infused, which absolutely precludes weariness ; their countenances exhibiting, rather the eagerness of youthful sport, than the labour of an imposed task.

5. **Unequal progress of different Scholars.** —This is an inconvenience so well known, and so generally felt, that it will be unnecessary to trouble the reader with any observation upon it. It will be enough to state the remedy

Unequal progress.

which Dr. Bell has applied.—At the time of getting their lessons, the class is paired off into pupils and tutors ; the head-boy taking care of the lowest, and shewing him the manner of learning his lesson ; and the boys next in succession, each taking a pupil in the same way. The lower boys have thus the most advantageous means of instruction; and the more intelligent have an opportunity of being prepared and fitted for teachers. It is indeed most delightful, to witness the willing spirit, with which the upper scholars undertake this task, the interest which they have in the progress of their pupils, and the mutual kindness which subsists between both. It will however happen that an idle or stupid boy cannot be so recovered, but that he impedes the progress of his class ; whilst, at the same time a clever lad, advanced before his fellows, is acquiring an habit of indolence, for want of sufficient occupation. If therefore a pupil remains at the bottom of his class, with evident marks of inferiority, he is removed to a lower form ; and on the other hand, if a boy continues at the head without a competitor, he is either appointed the teacher, or assistant teacher of his own class, or promoted to another, according to circumstances.

6. **The want of qualified and intelligent schoolmasters.**—This is a considerable bar to the extension of education. With the present demand for clerks and accountants, to manage the immense variety of commercial and colonial speculations, in this country and in others dependant on it, offering present emolument, and prospect of great advantages, there is nothing that can be attached to a parochial school, sufficient to retain a youth, who possesses any degree of intelligence, industry, and attention. They therefore, who can do better, quit the school for more profitable employment; and they, whom want of energy and inferiority of talent (I speak generally, and not with intent to censure) preclude from higher views, continue the pensioners of the public, until age and infirmities remove them.—

Masters.

Upon Dr. Bell's plan, a large school will, in a few months, supply an almost indefinite number of masters; to whom at their entrance on the stage of life, the most moderate salary will be an object ; until their habits and acquirements enable them to advance to a more lucrative situation, and they thus make room for a succession of other teachers equally prepared.

7. 𝕿𝖍𝖊 𝖜𝖆𝖓𝖙 𝖔𝖋 𝖉𝖎𝖘𝖈𝖎𝖕𝖑𝖎𝖓𝖊 𝖎𝖓 𝖑𝖆𝖗𝖌𝖊 𝖘𝖈𝖍𝖔𝖔𝖑𝖘.

Discipline.

—The impossibility that *one person* should constantly watch over the individual conduct of *many*, has hitherto put a limit to the number of scholars. Fifty boys have been considered as more than one master can manage : and where a school has been extended to 300 or 400 scholars, several masters and ushers have been required; great attention has been applied to their selection, and great expense incurred in their salaries and other incidental charges ; and, even when that has been ever so successfully done, the effect has been the same, as if in an army, the place of the many non-commission officers, were to be filled up by a few *field officers and generals.*—In Dr. Bell's schools, this part of the establishment is supplied by a number of monitors and teachers, rising spontaneously from among the boys themselves:—*non-commission officers,* selected without trouble, and serving without pay : a selection, which while it gives a spring of action to all the machinery of the school, supplies assistants much more capable of watching and managing their school-fellows; and much more interested in that discipline on which their own character and advancement depends; while they are managing and instructing others, they are acquiring the habit of teaching and conducting themselves.

8. 𝔗𝔥𝔢 𝔰𝔪𝔞𝔩𝔩 𝔫𝔲𝔪𝔟𝔢𝔯 𝔴𝔥𝔦𝔠𝔥 𝔞 𝔪𝔞𝔰𝔱𝔢𝔯 𝔠𝔞𝔫 𝔱𝔢𝔞𝔠𝔥 𝔦𝔫 𝔱𝔥𝔢 𝔠𝔬𝔪𝔪𝔬𝔫 𝔪𝔢𝔱𝔥𝔬𝔡.   Number of scholars.
—I am aware that there are individuals gifted with extraordinary powers of instruction. In general, however, these powers are very limited; and the examination of several pupils, by the master

alone, can never be made with any precision and certainty. The utmost that he can
do is to take the chance of detecting and
punishing negligence ; and the pupil is too
often willing to submit to what he considers
as a *mere chance* of detection and punishment.—In the new method, the increase of
number is so far from creating embarrass-
ment, that it supplies aid, and facilitates execution. The classes are better arranged,
the teachers more quickly prepared and
more easily selected, and the spur of emulation more effectually applied, than in a
smaller school. If a boy neglect his task,
he does not calculate on the *chance* of detection, but he feels the *certainty* of it; the
next boy below him who sets him right,
takes his place of course, by the known law
of the school, without any appeal to either
teacher or master.

9. 𝕿𝖍𝖊 𝖉𝖎𝖋𝖋𝖎𝖈𝖚𝖑𝖙𝖞 𝖔𝖋 𝖆𝖘𝖈𝖊𝖗𝖙𝖆𝖎𝖓𝖎𝖓𝖌 𝖙𝖍𝖊 𝖕𝖗𝖔=
Examination of   𝖌𝖗𝖊𝖘𝖘 𝖔𝖋 𝖆 𝖘𝖈𝖍𝖔𝖔𝖑.—The
progress.   usual mode is by personal
examination of the scholars. But without an

account of what they had previously learnt, and a statement of what they have been doing, it is hardly possible for the master, and it is utterly impossible for a stranger, to say what has been the real progress of any school in any certain period.—The register which Dr. Bell has adopted, of the lessons of the several classes, is so effectual and complete, that by referring to it, any visitor may, at any time, see what progress each class has made in any given period; and, seeing that, he may try in different instances, whether their improvement is real and permanent. This register is simple, and easily kept by the little teacher of each class; who regularly makes his entry of the lessons learnt, previously to his going out of the school.—

THE statement which I here offer to the reader, has been prepared chiefly from what I have myself observed * in the new schools. There are several improvements, such as *writing*

Practices.

* Many who have written on Dr. Bell's system, have taken their ideas from books, rather than from

in sand, syllabic reading, and unreiterated spelling, very useful, but not essential parts of the system. The writing * in sand is

practical observations on what passed in his schools. It has been supposed that he discarded all corporal punishment. This is not so ; nor has he instead of it (as has been also supposed) adopted degrading, capricious, or ridiculous punishments. The black book and trial by jury have also been considered as objectionable.—In Dr. Bell's schools, the rod is not absolutely proscribed, but it is rendered unnecessary : no instance of the use of it has come within my knowledge. I observe that the black book is hardly known ; and when called for, it is *ut metus ad omnes, pœna ad paucos perveniat.* In those cases the severe justice of the jury was not relaxed on their part, but was mitigated by the power of mercy vested in the master.

† It has been conceived that Dr. Bell proposed to limit the education of the poor to *reading* only ; and a reference has been made to the following passage in his last work called, " *The Madras School.*"—" It is not proposed that the children of the poor be edu-" cated in an expensive manner, or *all of them* taught to " write and to cypher ;"—and the inference drawn by some persons has been, that he did not wish *any of the poor* to be taught to write and to cypher.—The inference, however, which I draw, is that Dr. Bell, soliciting for such an universal education for the poor as should enable them all to read their bible, did not venture to push his request so far, that *all* the poor, every poor person in this kingdom, every individual in the cottage, should be taught to *write and cypher* at the public expense—a consummation which he desires, and which I hope and trust will *eventually* take place in this country ; so that

taken from *writing on the ground*, which is no modern invention, but an oriental practice of remote antiquity. It supplies, however, interesting means of instruction for the youngest pupils. I have frequently been extremely gratified by the pleasure, rapidity, and accuracy, with which a little child will learn his letters in this playful way ; and I have been surprised to see how soon it becomes his amusement, and wins and engages his whole attention. There are also great advantages in syllabic * reading, and un-

the benefits of the *alphabetical and numerical language* may be enjoyed by every one of our fellow subjects.—If he had meant otherwise, of what use would have been his directions for writing in sand, his chapter upon writing, and another upon arithmetic, or the instruction he gives on those subjects in his schools? With these circumstances before us, can we suppose that because he did not *hope* that *all* the poor would have the advantage of writing and cyphering, he did not *wish* that *any* of them, or even that the great majority of them, should possess those advantages?

* In Dr. Bell's schools, the visitor will find several things which at first view will appear to him objectionable, but which, upon an attentive observation of their effects, he will find reason to approve. Such is the syllabic spelling, in the manner it is taught; that is with great exertion of voice applied to each individual

reiterated spelling; and in the clear and *vociferous* pronunciation of every syllable; which though not very grateful to a fastidious ear, gives a distinctness of articulation,* peculiar to the *new school.* These however, are only to be styled *practices,* and enter as auxiliaries into a system, of which they are independent.† The grand principle

syllable. This is at first grating to the ear; but it is the cause of that peculiar pronunciation which distinguishes Dr. Bell's scholars. It eventually produces distinctness of articulation, without effort or unnatural tone.—This is one of many proofs, that Dr. Bell's improvements are the result of inquiry and experiment.

* Among other advantages from distinctness and slowness of articulation, and the several syllables being successively given, and each word being read by a different pupil, is to be stated the cure of *stammering* in speech. Mr. Smith, the Master of the Blue Coat School at Auckland, mentioned to me, that three of his boys, whose articulation was imperfect and accompanied with hesitation, were very nearly cured of this defect in the course of three weeks, by the practice of reading loudly and distinctly, *each a separate word in his turn:* I heard one of them read, and from my own observation can confirm Mr. Smith's statement. The other two boys were not then in the school.

† For a more extended detail on Dr. Bell's system, the reader is referred to his " Elements of Tuition," and to his " Instructions for Conducting a School, &c." Both are sold by Hatchard.

of Dr. Bell's system, is THE DIVISION OF LABOUR, applied to *intellectual* purposes. The objects are " to continue attention with- " out weariness;—to quit nothing, until it " is distinctly and permanently fixed in the " mind,—and to make the pupils, the instru- " ments of their own instruction."

THE man who first made a practical use of the *division of labour*, gave a new power to the

Division of labour.

application of corporal strength, and simpli- fied and facilitated the most irksome and laborious operations. To him we are in- debted for " the greatest improvement in " the productive powers of labour, and for " the greater part of the skill, dexterity, " and judgment, with which it is any where " directed or applied."* But that man, whatever was his merit, did not more essen- tial service to *mechanical*, than Dr. Bell has done to *intellectual* operations. It is the divi- sion of labour in his schools, that leaves the master the easy task of directing the move-

* Smith on the Wealth of Nations.

ments of the whole machine, instead of toiling ineffectually at a single part. The principle in manufactories, and in schools is the same. The practical application, in each instance, has required the same acuteness and perseverance of mind, to correct the wanderings of theory * and conjecture, by repeated trial and continued attention.

THE discovery of Dr. BELL is not less
Benefits of the new   the production of a philo-
method.   sophic mind, or less the
effect of science working by experiment, than that of Mr. DAVY on alkalies, or Dr. JENNER † on vaccination.—Consider for a

---

* I hardly ever knew a visitor to Dr. Bell's school, who did not at first entertain doubts as to parts of his system : and yet I have never seen an instance, where the visitor possessed any degree of candour and attention, that he did not afterwards acknowledge things at first apparently and theoretically wrong, to have been, upon investigation, essentially and practically right. This affords additional proof that the system is the result of experiment, and not of accidental discovery.

† We know how to value the experiments on VAC-CINATION, which DR. JENNER continued with patient and persevering attention, for above twenty years. We revere that anxiety of mind, which, labouring to confer

moment, what it is to have removed the
principal impediments to the acquisition of
elementary knowledge,—to have rendered
that discipline easy and pleasant, which we
remember in youth to have been hard and
offensive,——and to have accustomed the
rising generation to avoid what is *imperfect
and superficial,**—the perpetual source of
an unqualified blessing on his species, produced it perfect
and entire, like Minerva from the head of Jupiter ;—
and displayed it so clearly and luminously, that the
most ignorant practitioners thought themselves at once
the complete masters of the subject ; and some even
persuaded themselves, and endeavoured to persuade the
public, *that they understood the discovery better than even
Jenner himself.*—With regard to the other respected
name which I have mentioned ;—in his experiments on
alkalies,—in reducing them to their component parts,
and in recomposing and restoring the entire body,
hitherto an inscrutable object of science, and in his subsequent experiments on acids and earths, Mr. Davy
has, indeed, proceeded with unexampled rapidity. But
this has been the result of long and deep anterior study
and meditation, the effect of extreme exertion that
nearly cost his life, the act of one who has been engaged
in philosophical investigation from his youth —In the
course of a life *happily employed,* it is no small gratification to me to number among *my most intimate friends,*
the three individuals, to whose discoveries I have now
referred.

* The principles of Dr. Bell's system, are applicable

error and vice ;—and to consider nothing as learnt, that is not clearly, distinctly, and permanently fixed in the mind.

A defect in the old mode of education is, Defects of the old that it employs many in-structors and great ex-pense, to produce small and inconsiderable effects ; and that it *teaches* every thing, but does not allow the pupil to acquire any thing of himself ; confining him in the per-petual *go-cart of tuition*, and precluding him from the habit of using and exercising his own faculties.   It is thus, that general and vague ideas are infused into the mind on all subjects, without any thing precise or per-manent being obtained on any ; and it is thus that a kind of *bird's-eye view* of the arts and sciences is offered to the intellect, with-

to the highest attainments of elevated rank, as well as to the humblest proficiency in elementary knowledge. The time, I trust, is not far distant, when it will be applied in such a way, as to induce mothers to *condescend* to be the superintendants of their own nurseries, and to enable the elder daughters to be the governesses and teachers of their younger sisters.

out any fixed or distinct knowledge of any of them.—

THE dissenters of every sect are at present actively and honour- Activity of the ably employed* in the work dissenters. of education. Their labours are not confined to their own members, but are extended to other societies of Christians, not excluding the poor of the established church.

* It is very well known, (says Dr. Haygarth), that various classes of dissenters, with enthusiastic diligence, are teaching the lower classes of children to read, &c. in great numbers, through most parts of England. The question therefore now is, not whether this instruction should be given to them at all, but by whom? under the direction of the church of England, or of sectaries?—Last August (1807) being at Rodborough, in Gloucestershire, I inquired what effect had been produced upon the behaviour of the inhabitants, by the introduction of machinery into the woollen manufactures of that valley, fearing to receive a very unfavourable report. But I was informed that the poor manufacturers had lately become much more orderly, sober, and industrious: and as a proof of the truth of this remark, the landlord of the Inn assured me that he now sold 300*l.* worth less ale and spirits in a year, than he had done fourteen years ago. This change in the behaviour and morals of the people, he wholly ascribed to the effect of their education by the dissenters.—Dr. Haygarth's Letter to the Bishop of London.

There are some persons, who now dread their active zeal, their indefatigable industry, and their unceasing activity, in the propagation of tenets, which it is but christian candour to suppose, they think conducive, if not essential, to salvation. If this is a time for apprehension, what must we look forward to, if we do not now supply all our own poor with the inestimable benefit of education? What must we expect if we leave part of them without instruction, and part to receive it from other hands? What must be the effect, when in a very few years, myriads of our children, indebted to sectaries for the advantages of education, shall enter on the stage of life;— more instructed, more informed, and more animated by religious zeal and ardour, than the ignorant and untaught members of our own church! If the outworks of the establishment appear to the timid mind to be now in danger, what arms will then be found to defend the citadel against such numerous and powerful assailants?

It is not one of the least advantages which

will be derived from our
own clergy taking the lead
in the new system of education (a system, I
should observe, originating from one of their
own members, and fostered in the very
bosom of the church), that the selection of
books * for the pupils, will be in the hands
of the friends to religion, morality, and civil
order.   At the time of the French revolu-
tion, the greatest danger that existed, was

Selections of books.

* To such subscribers to " the Society for promoting
" Christian Knowledge," as are desirous of supplying
books to their poor neighbours, and to schools in their
vicinage; I beg leave to recommend the following list
of 2150 books, the expense of which will be FIVE
GUINEAS.

300	Child's first Book, Part I.	o	14	3
300	Ditto, Part II.	o	14	3
400	Ostervald's Abridgement of the Bible,	o	14	0
400	Chief Truths of Religion,	o	12	0
100	Catechism broken into Questions,	o	7	6
200	Our Saviours Sermon on the Mount,	o	8	0
170	The Order of Confirmation,	o	8	0
100	Trimmer's Spelling Book for Boys,	o	8	0
50	Ditto for Girls,	o	4	0
100	Ditto, Part II.	o	12	0
30	Bishop Wilson's Prayers,	o	2	6
		5	5	0

The Subscription to the Society is One Guinea a Year.

from the pernicious falsities, which were industriously circulated among the poor. That
power is still in existence ; and the most
pernicious effects might be produced by dis-
seminating false principles of conduct, and
habituating the mind to scenes of debased
sensuality or unfeeling barbarity.

THERE are few who have not felt the
Danger from im- truth of what LONGINUS has
proper books. said *on the sublime ;*—that
" it habituates the soul to grandeur, and
" impregnates it with generous and enlarged
" ideas." By studies of this kind the intellectual powers are purified and strengthened,
and the soul acquires a foretaste and preparation for spiritual existence. As these improve, so do books of a contrary tendency
degrade and enfeeble the faculties. The
mind which has fed on licentious description,
—on narratives of cruelty,—or on false
morals, becomes diseased and corrupted by
the noxious food. In mature life these are,
indeed, the consequences of depraved habits.
I leave to him, who can *sate himself upon*

celestial food, and *prey on garbage*, to select studies congenial to his own feelings. No eye was ever gratified by scenes of barbarity,—no ear by descriptions of licentiousness,—no mind by display of corrupt principles of action,—unless the taste for evil had been first established in the heart, by the destruction of the higher and nobler feelings of man. I therefore do not refer myself to mature life, but to youth;—to those, whose principles and habits do still depend on the communication which they receive. To them, I say, it is of the utmost importance, that the books which are placed in their hands, shall be correct in principle, and pure in respect of religion and morality.

AS to the funds requisite for an universal system of education, I feel no anxiety. Upon the plan *Funds for education.* adopted in Chester, and at Auckland ;* our

* The following are the queries, as to the endowed and other schools in this diocese, which the Bishop of Durham has recently circulated in his Bishoprick :— 1. What schools are there in your parish and immediate neighbourhood ; and what is the nature and

endowed charity schools, without at all interfering with the original objects, would supply a great part of what is wanted ; especially upon Dr. Bell's plan, which reduces the expense of a day school to a mere trifle. At the same time, one cannot too much deplore the timidity or supineness of those, who with a conviction of existing abuses, omit to direct a general and national inquiry, into the present state of SCHOOL ENDOWMENTS, AND OTHER CHARITIES :* an inquiry, which

amount of their respective funds? 2. What is the average number of children which have been educated in such schools respectively, for the three preceding years ; and how many of them have been clothed, and how many clothed and boarded ? 3. How far are such schools adequate to the education of all, or what proportion of the children in the several places where they are situated ? 4. Are you of opinion that any practicable improvement, or extension of the beneficial effects of any such schools can be adopted, consistently with the terms of the original foundation ?

* In the first volume of the Society's Reports, I offered some remarks on the situation of charitable endowments in this country, and referred to the Report of the Committee of the House of Commons of the 10th of June, 1788. In this Report, it is stated that " many charitable donations have been lost ; and many " others, from neglect of payment, and the inattention " of those persons who ought to superintend them, are

would immediately induce the parties to bring their funds into action ; convinced that if they omit to correct what is amiss, they might soon be reminded of their duty by THE LORD CHANCELLOR.

BEFORE I quit my subject, I cannot help wishing to place before the The situation of the view of the reader the situa- uneducated labourer· tion of the *uneducated labourer*, in the different periods of life; requesting him to consider how far the condition of such an individual is, or is not, favourable to the permanency of civil society.—In childhood, his mind is vacant, unoccupied, and exposed to every baneful impression and noxious

---

" in danger of being lost, or rendered very difficult to be " recovered."— It also appears by the Report, that the rental of those estates, that consisted of land only, without the personal funds, amounted to above 210,cool. a year at that time, being now twenty years ago.   The Report concludes with observing that " this is a matter " of such *magnitude*, as to call for the SERIOUS AND " SPEEDY ATTENTION of Parliament."—Twenty years have since passed,—twice the period of the Trojan war,—without this *serious and speedy attention of Parliament*, having as yet been given.

example. In mature age, the want of mental and domestic resources is supplied by the society of the alehouse, and by pugilistic sports : and in declining life, when, the body becomes languid and stiff, and the powers of active labour cease,—when, in the other classes of life, intellectual pleasure supplies, *or should supply*, the place of sensual gratification,—the poor sufferer drags on a weary and comfortless existence ; and totters to the confines of an eternity, for which he has had no means of preparation. Look to his hours of rest from daily labour, or to the weekly return of his Sabbath, you will find that those intervals, which might have been so happily employed in the instruction of his children, and in domestic intercourse,—in contemplating the great scheme of redemption,* in preparing the

* One of my great objects has always been to place THE BIBLE in the hands of every poor man, and to enable him to read it.—Upon this subject, I have real pleasure in quoting the authority of BISHOP WARBURTON, in his seventeenth Letter to BISHOP HURD : " Take" (says he) " a plain man, with an honest heart ; " give him his BIBLE, and make him conversant in it, " and I will engage for him, *he will never be at a loss to*

minds of others for the same contemplation,
—and in supplying sources of meditation for
his solitary hours,—have been to him dark,
—comfortless,—and disastrous;

> ———— from the cheerful ways of men
> Cut off, and for the book of knowledge fair,
> Presented with an universal blank.

IN settled times, the power of the law
and the dread of punish-   In time of comment, may to a certain de-   motion.
gree, deter from crimes.*   But in political
commotions, the *uneducated pauper* has neither principle nor motive, to induce him to
respect or defend that state of society, the
benefits whereof he has not been taught to
appreciate. He is prepared for any alteration
in the state of things, fearless of change, and
indifferent as to consequences.

WHEN I add that this description does
Want of education   not entirely apply to the
in Ireland.   present state of England,

* " *know how to act, agreeably to his duty, in every circum-*
" *stance of life.*"

I wish it were in my power to say as much of Ireland. But, all our danger from that quarter, all the evils which we have suffered, and all that we have to apprehend, all the miseries under which that country has laboured, and all the impediments to its improvement, are occasioned by our not having made any proper and effectual provision* for the instruction and civilization of the Irish poor.

IN the Reports † of the Society, an example has been offered of a nation purified and corrected by the single remedy of education. Infested by mendicity, and by all the evils

Effects of it in Scotland.

---

* Nothing would so effectually contribute to the improvement, if not to the conversion of the Irish Roman Catholics, as the general diffusion of moral and religious instruction among them. An enlightened and virtuous Christian can never be a *bigotted* papist.—With regard to the Charter-schools in Ireland, I have been very much misinformed, if the impolitic and intolerant condition, on which education in them is given to the catholic poor, contributes so much to conversion, as to violent and bitter prejudice against the established church.

† See Report, No. CXXVIII An extract from it will be inserted in a subsequent part of this volume.

and vices which appertain to the association of thousands of mendicants, defying the laws of God and man, because hopeless of benefit under them,—a single Act of the Parliament of Scotland, *providing instruction for all the children of the poor*, did in the lapse of a few passing years, administer a perfect and lasting remedy for the greatest political evil, by which a community can be afflicted. The national disease was not only cured; but from the period of the operation of that act, the peasantry in Scotland has stood on higher ground, and has possessed a more elevated scale of character, than in any other part of the world.

In contradiction, however, to the effects which have been ascribed to the universality of educa- Objections to the account. tion in Scotland, it has been observed that, in this country, simplicity of character, and purity of morals have not gone hand in hand with the progress of education. It has been stated that, though more has been done during the last ten years, towards forming

and establishing schools for the poor in this
kingdom, than in any age or country during
the same period, yet license and luxury are
pervading every class and every village in
the kingdom ; and are corrupting and destroying the habits and principles, not merely
of the rich and idle, but of the poor and
laborious.

THOSE, however, who hold this language (and there are some
Answer to them.
who hold it with sincerity,
and really believe what they assert) con-
found the medicine with the disease, and
impute pernicious effects to their only effectual remedy.—It is no novelty in the world,
that immoderate wealth and power, should
corrupt the individuals, and destroy the nations, by which they are possessed. The
greatest, the firmest, and the most compact
fabrics of empire which the world has beheld, have successively sunk under their own
weight ; and have perished, not by *the poison
of education*, but for want of its renovating
power ;—for want of the sole and efficacious

remedy, which, supplying principles, and motives, and habits, counteracts the evils attendant on inordinate prosperity.

IF other commercial states,—if other mighty empires, have been weighed down by the bur- Political situation. then of the rich and splendid ornaments with which they have been incumbered, how is Britain to plead exemption ? What is left but EDUCATION, to preserve her from the effects of a rapid and unceasing influx of wealth from both the Indies ?—from the consequences of boundless and lucrative speculations in every part of the globe ?— and from the influence of manufactories,*

* The moral and political remedy, which the paro- chial schools in Scotland, do now supply for the evils and inconvenience of the manufactures of that part of the island, was ably stated by the Lord Justice, at the Circuit Court of Glasgow, on the 29th of April, 1808 ; an extract from his Lordship's speech, stating unequivocally and unexceptionably the advantages of general instruc- tion, and the remedial effects of education for those evils which are inseparable from the prosperous state of civil society, will be given in a note, in a subsequent part of this volume.

which congregate legions of the rising generation, disciplined only to watch and direct
their machinery, but neglected and forgotten
as to every privilege and distinction of a
rational and immortal being? What is to
preserve us during a war, which we have
been compelled to wage for many years,
by which the manners of a camp are extended to every remote and retired corner of
the island,—and the young labourer is taught
the vices of a soldier, before he can benefit
by his discipline and essential virtues?

WITH such abundant sources of corruption, where can the patriot
Call for education.
who desires the happiness,
or even the existence of his country,—where
can he look for security, to what can he
direct his hopes, but to EDUCATION,—formed
on the general principles of Christianity,—
bestowed impartially upon all our fellow
subjects,—and connected in amity * with our
civil and religious establishment?

* When I speak of a national system of education,
" connected in *amity* with our religious establishment,"

I FEAR I may have trespassed on the patience of my reader ; but

Conclusion.

I claim something for the nature of my subject ; which by those who take a real interest in it, is considered, and I trust will be admitted, to be one of the most important, which can engage the human mind. It is not a question about the preference of a philosophic theory or literary discussion ;—but it involves the *temporal* welfare and utility, and the *eternal happiness*, of millions. It is, whether under the CHRISTIAN DISPENSATION, knowledge shall be confined to a favoured class ; and whether we, who enjoy the spontaneous and impartial bounty of heaven, shall withhold the blessings of instruction from the

and while I wish it to receive the aid, and to be under the direction of that establishment, I do not mean that the system shall be made subservient to its power, or instrumental of conversion to its tenets.—To deal out EDUCATION TO THE POOR only on the terms of *religious conformity*, is, in my opinion, a species of persecution ; differing not greatly from the supplying of bread to the hungry and necessitous, on similar conditions,— and being as defective in true policy, as it is unjust in principle.

great mass of our fellow subjects? It is whether our countrymen shall be noxious examples of misery and ignorance, corrected and restrained only by capital punishments, or whether they shall be made happy and useful in this world, and prepared to look with hope and humble confidence to another?

THOMAS BERNARD.

26 Jan. 1809.

OBSERVATIONS

ON THE

EDUCATION OF THE POOR.

SELECTED

FROM THE REPORTS

OF THE SOCIETY.

OBSERVATIONS, &c.

T H E true application of CHARITY,* like perfect knowledge in metaphysics, seems to have
been left as a subject of indefinite research and
inquiry; in order that the faculties of man
might be stimulated and exercised with more
earnest attention, to its perfection, and to his
own improvement. If, indeed, this science
were easily to be acquired, and the bearings,
the limits, and the boundaries, precisely and
correctly ascertained, one of the most potent incentives to benevolent researches would cease;
the kind and amiable affections of the heart
might lose their influence; and every sentiment, congenial with charity, might stagnate in

* See Introductory Letter to the third volume of the
Reports.

torpid inactivity. In this, however, as in other objects of inquiry, while the distant undis-covered country of speculation rises in clouds before us, it is always in our power to know as much, as can be *practically* useful. So much, in any event, we may clearly discover, that whatever encourages and promotes habits of industry, prudence, foresight, virtue, and clean-liness among the poor, is beneficial to them and to the country ;—whatever removes or dimi-nishes the incitement to any of these qualities, is detrimental to the State, and pernicious to the individual. This is the POLAR STAR of our benevolent affections ; directing them to their true end,—and preserving them, not only from that capricious selection of objects, which, un-just in principle and injurious in effect, seeks rather to gratify personal whim and distem-pered humour, than to promote the well-being of its fellow creatures ; but also from that in-discriminate and undirected bounty, which may " give all its goods to feed the poor," and yet possess no one individual characteristic, or pro-perty, of genuine and useful charity —

The only rational hope of diminishing our present parochial burthens, and of affording a remedy to those evils which are incident to

populous and opulent states, must be founded
on the success of measures for *bettering the condition of the poor.*   It must be by the education
of youth, by the moral and religious habits of
mature age, by the improvement of the cottager's means of life, by the increase of his resources, and of his habits of industry and foresight,—by these means, and by these only, that
the condition of the poor can ever be essentially
and permanently improved,—the prosperity of
the country augmented,—and the parochial
burthens eventually diminished. Without these
means, workhouses, and alms-houses, public
edifices, and hospitals, may be erected with increasing and unwearied diligence throughout
the land, and yet never keep pace with the
progress of indigence and misery.

It cannot* be too often repeated, that to
promote virtue and good habits among our
fellow subjects, rewards and incitements must
be made use of; that, though punishment and
terror may deter from criminal and atrocious
actions ; yet, to produce in the cottager a superior tone of conduct,—to give existence to any
degree of exertion and prudence beyond the

* Observations on Report, No. LI.

common line of mediocrity,—and to impress
in the mind, and fix indelibly in the heart,
regular and principled habits of life,—reward,
commendation, and encouragement, are necessary. Indeed, if we would preserve those
blessings which Providence has bestowed on
this favoured island, it is necessary that the
higher classes of society should be immediately
awakened to the duty of assisting, by every
exertion in their power, the prevalence of industry, prudence, morality, and religion, among
the great mass of our fellow subjects. To this
desired effect, disinterested kindness, and well
directed encouragement, are indispensible re-
quisites. Without them, words and actions are
but empty professions ; and the poor and uneducated cottager will never profitably receive
that instruction, which is not enforced by the
example of the teacher.

It is the misfortune of this country, and it
has been the calamity, and it may prove the
destruction, of Ireland, that the different classes
of society have not a sufficient bond and connection of intercourse ;—that they want that frequent communication of kindness and benefit,
and that reciprocal good will and esteem,
which (except only in the case of the worst of

beings) must always result from rational creatures possessing the means of knowing, and
appreciating. each other's good qualities and
utility.   When that does not take place, the
unfortunate consequence is, that neither of the
parties does justice to the other.   The rich do
not sufficiently estimate the virtues and suffer-
ings of the poor: nor are the latter aware of
the real and affectionate interest, which *many
of the higher classes in England* feel in their
welfare.   This, however, is not all:—The rich
become less useful, because they under value
their own influence and power of doing good:
and the poor are often degraded in their own
opinion, and debased in character, by the persuasion, that they neither possess, or are entitled
to, the esteem and regard of the other ranks
in life.

The scarcity of wheat corn in the two preceding winters, contributed to remove, for a
time, those unjust and injurious prejudices.
But that effect cannot be permanent, without
some attention and exertion on the part of the
rich: and in no way can they employ that attention and exertion better, than by bestowing
publicly, and in the face of the country, praise
and reward to the good conduct of the poor;

and by raising a spirit of virtuous and honourable emulation among them.

To these suggestions on the encouragement to be given to the virtues of the poor, and on the intercourse of kindness which should take place between them and the rich, I shall offer a few observations, which apply to the sub-ject of charity in general.—In the conduct of every charitable fund, it is very essential, that we should have in view the rule adopted at Hamburgh,—" that if the manner, in which " relief is given, is not a spur to industry, it " becomes, in effect, a premium to sloth and " profligacy."—All the evils that did attend the indiscriminate charity of our religious foun-dations before the Reformation, when the idle and the profligate had always a monastic gate, where they might apply for that food, which they ought to have procured by their own in-dustry,—a time, when the nerves and sinews of the country were relaxed and debilitated, by the warmth of misapplied charity,—all those evils which then existed, must at this, and at every period, attend the unwise and capricious administration of relief to the necessitous : and it is not merely that those who are relieved, are thereby rendered indolent and helpless, but

the spirit of the other poor is *blighted* by the
sight of thriving idleness and successful imposture, and their energy and vigour are ener-
vated by the tender of gratuitous and unmerited
relief.

Some pious persons, in the distribution of
charity, regard the motive rather than the end ;
not being sufficiently aware that, in removing
the incitement to industry, they are frequently
doing much more injury, than benefit, to the
objects of their bounty.—But I forbear to enter
into a detail of the evils that attend the encouragement of mendicity. There is no beggar
who is not really entitled to our compassion ;
—from the well dressed *Asker*, who approaches
you with an easy air of confidence and fami-
liarity,—to the wretched object, who trusts for
his support to the display of filth and misery,
too disgusting and too offensive for the human
eye to endure. And if this source of public
benevolence, however misdirected, were at any
period to be hastily checked, before there shall
be opened in the metropolis, for their support
and amendment, that public asylum, which
both policy and charity require, and which
I at present can only anticipate in expectation,
numbers of these unhappy creatures must

perish in the streets, or by the hands of the
executioner.

Without inquiring what appropriations of
benevolence are in their effects destructive of
prudence and industry among the poor, I shall
proceed to enumerate those charities, the good
effects whereof are unqualified and unquestion-
able.—These are, such as prepare and fit children for an useful situation in life ;—such as
assist and promote industry, prudence, and
domestic economy in the cottages of the poor;
—or which, in cases of public or private misfortune, prevent their domestic plan of economy
from being destroyed ;—and lastly, such as
openly and publicly offer reward and encouragement to the virtues and good conduct
of the poor.

In the first rank may be placed those institutions, which contribute to educate and improve
the rising generation, and to fit them for their
station in life, and for useful employment ;—
that instruct them in the great and important
duties of christianity, and form their minds at
an early period, to strict and principled habits
of integrity and prudence. While these charities have their full effect, we need never despair
of our country ; but may look with confidence

to a renewal of strength and virtue, in the succession of honest and industrious youth.

To occupy life * with satisfaction,—to improve the morals, and increase the happiness,
of the circle around us,—to strengthen the
bonds, and insure the peace, of society,—and
to draw gratitude and blessings from a virtuous
and thriving neighbourhood,—these are not
pleasures of an ordinary cast, or of inferior consideration. These enjoyments, however, and
more than these, may be attained by those individuals, who may be induced to follow the examples which have been detailed in the Reports,
and to form themselves into societies for the
protection and improvement of the poor. Great
indeed would be the benefit of such associations,
for the assistance of middle age, for the relief
and consolation of declining years, and for that
object, the importance of which cannot be too
strongly or too frequently stated,—*the education of youth* in steady habits of industry and
integrity, and in the genuine principles of
christianity.

Of EDUCATION it may be truly said, that it is
the only earthly blessing, capable of being uni-

* Observations on Report, No. LXIV.

versally diffused and enjoyed, with an exemption from all inconvenient consequences. I
speak of that genuine and well directed education, which is calculated to fit persons to act a
strenuous and useful part, in their allotted
station in life ;—of that education, which
teaches and demonstrates the advantages of
early and steady habits of attention and industry, and forms in the heart, stable and permanent principles of conduct. It is this, and
this only, which supplying the mind with competent funds of human knowledge, and with
just conceptions of man's probationary state in
this world, drawn from the sources of revelation, doth thereby preserve it from the danger
and *taint* of infidelity ; that never confidently
attempts, and very rarely succeeds in debasing
and corrupting the heart of man, unless where
it has been left vacant and unoccupied, for the
evil spirit to fix his abode in.

In the present state of Ireland, and (to take
a wider and more awful scope) amid the tre-
mendous convulsions which have for some time
agitated Europe, let us reflect how much of the
evil is to be attributed to *an improvident neglect in the education of the poor ;* a neglect,
which has left them a defenceless prey to the

sophistry and delusion of the teachers of infidelity, and of the disseminators of sedition. Ignorant, unprincipled, incapable of giving a reason for their faith, or of explaining the benefits of civil order and society, to what miseries have not the poor, in many parts of Europe, been exposed? How have they been taught, by sad and calamitous experience, that without the sanctions of revealed religion, and the restrictions of civil polity, man is, of all animals, the most savage and noxious? and that reason, which is his boast and pride, (and justly so when properly directed) becomes in a perverted state, the potent instrument of evil; and enables him to surpass the ferocious beast, and the venemous animal, in the magnitude and extent of the calamities, too often inflicted on his fellow creatures.

Every attainment of man carries in it the principle of decay and corruption; with exception only of that instruction and institution, which prepares him for the performance of duty here, and for the enjoyment of happiness hereafter. Of manufactures, of commerce, of both individual and national prosperity, nay, even of science itself, the extended and abundant increase tends to complete the fatal circle ; and, by decay, convulsion, anarchy, and misery, to produce a new and renovated order of things. In an advanced state of society, where the meridian is attained or passed, nothing can prevent or even protract the evil day, except the revivifying influence of education, operating to correct the vices which flow from affluence and prosperity.

To England, in its present state, these considerations are of peculiar importance. While increasing streams of wealth pour into this country from every part of the globe, it behoves us, if we would guard against the pernicious effects of corrupt and luxurious habits, anxiously to attend to the education of the children of the poor. Without that care, we we may read our history, in that of the many rich and prosperous empires, which have preceded us. On the contrary, while the religious education of the great mass of the people is duly and successfully attended to, and they are prepared in their turn to reap and enjoy the benefits of active industry and useful economy, we need never (to repeat the words of a former report) " despair of our country ; but may

" look with confidence to a renewal of strength
" and virtue, in the succession of honest and
" industrious youth."

In a subsequent part of this volume, we shall
offer examples of different institutions for the
instruction and improvement of youth. Of
day schools, the first in order of communication upon our Reports, is that of the REV. MR.
GILPIN, at BOLDRE,* for twenty boys and
twenty girls; of which, though instruction is
the chief object, industry is blended with it.
After a judicious and liberal support of these
schools during his life, the excellent founder
has constituted a permanent endowment for
them, by appropriating to their support, the
produce of his drawings, and of some other of
his works.—The next in the Reports † offers
the example of an extensive and noble range of
religious and moral discipline, in the MENDIP
SCHOOLS; extending over twelve parishes, dispersed through a district of country of about
twenty-five miles in diameter, and founded
and supported by the active and unremitting
zeal of MISS HANNAH MORE, and her sister.
—The KENDAL SCHOOLS,‡ established by DR.

* Reports, No. XXXV.   † Ibid, No. LXIV.
‡ Ibid, No. XC.

BRIGGS, unite industry with education, and
are remarkable for supplying one of the first
examples of the adoption of the REV. DR.
BELL's mode of instruction, in this country.
The schools for eighty children, at WES-
TON, near Bath, established by the late Mrs.
HOCKER, and since her death continued by
two benevolent sisters, are distinguishable for
the tender age at which children are admitted
into them, and for the striking mode in which
their religious instruction has been supplied.
—In the fifth example of the WEST STREET
SCHOOLS,* the call for such a school in such
a neighbourhood as St. Giles's, and the difficulties which necessarily arose from the characters to be dealt with, have made the regularity, subordination, and improvement of
the children the more remarkable ; especially
since the number has been increased from
two hundred and forty children to about four
hundred,—all rescued from dangerous example
and helpless ignorance.—MR. LANCASTER's
schools in the Borough, the next in the Reports,†
but prior in time, afford an extraordinary
example of what may be done by a single individual, with very slender means. Without

* Reports, No. C.   † Ibid, No. CXVIII.

the aid of connections, or wealth, or classical
education, he has contrived to supply as many
as *a thousand children* with useful instruction,
at the price of seven shillings and sixpence a
year, as there stated; but since reduced to
about half that sum.——For the school at CAMP-
SALL,* in Yorkshire; the public is indebted
to three young ladies, the Miss FRANKS; who
have for some years, and at some expense, devoted their time and attention with great effect,
to the promotion of the industry, and moral
and religious improvement, of their poor neighbours.——For the account,† and indeed for the
formation of the school at DINAPORE, in the
East Indies, we are indebted to a lady, who in
conjunction with her sister, has not long since
laboured very successfully in the instruction of
the poor at Bridgenorth, in Shropshire. The
account of this school in HIS MAJESTY's
53d Regiment at Dinapore, is the more valuable, because it offers an unexceptionable example of instruction for the children of soldiers
in the different regiments on our establishment;
an example calculated to supply those children

* Reports, No. CXXV.

† This account has been recently received, and is now first
published.

with moral and religious principles,—to be acceptable to the parent,—gratifying to the pious philanthropist,—and beneficial to the country.

We shall offer to the reader, six examples of schools of industry;—at OAKHAM, LEWISHAM, HAMBURGH, FINCHAM, BIRMINGHAM,* and CHELTENHAM: and two of Sunday schools; the first at KIRKSTALL, in Yorkshire, and the second at DROMORE,† in Ireland, which will be the object of some observations peculiarly applicable to that country. To this we shall add an account of what have been already noticed in the Preface, the united schools at CHESTER,‡ and of an interesting and valuable Institution § for the education and employment of the FEMALE POOR.—Whether we look to its objects or advantages,—to its benefits or motives,—to the high and elevated characters which conduct it, or to injured and helpless individuals who are to receive relief from it,— it is indeed of the highest importance, that the energy and activity of this Committee should

---

* See Reports, Nos. IV, XXIX, XXXVII, CXII, and CXXIII.—The account of the Cheltenham school is now first published.

† Ibid, No. CXI and CXLII.   ‡ Ibid, No. LXI.

§ Ibid, No. CVIII

be exerted to the utmost practicable and unexceptionable degree.

These accounts will be followed by an extract of the parochial returns,* lately made with regard to the state of education in IREDAND. The subject itself is interesting; but the time and the peculiar circumstances under which those returns have been made, considerably increase that interest.—A state † of the parochial schools of SCOTLAND, and copies of the Scotch acts of parliament, and of those of our late province of Massachuset's Bay, on education, (laws that have produced such an extraordinary distinction and superiority of character in those individuals, which have been blessed by them) is intended to form the next articles in this collection.—The rewards ‡ of the day school at Campsall, and the regulations of the school at St. John's Chapel, Bedford Row, with the Rev. Mr. Cecil's excellent address § to the parents of the scholars,—the advice to the Foundling children on their entrance into life,—a proposed inquiry ||

* Reports, No. CXVII.

† Ibid, No. CXXVIII, vol. v. Appendix, No. XIX, and vol. iii. Appendix, No. X.

‡ Ibid, vol. v. Appendix, No. IV.

§ These two are now first printed by the Society.

|| Reports, vol. iv. Appendix, No. IV. and XII.

into the present state of schools for the education
of the poor,—together with a little narrative
(now first published) looking chiefly to a practical exemplification of the manner of intro-
ducing into cottages and villages those improvements, which may tend to better the condition
and character of the poor ;—these will supply
the residue of a publication, which is submitted
to the reader, in the humble and unalloyed
hope, of its being useful to the great and most
numerous class of our fellow subjects.

If the * excellent example of the BISHOP OF
DROMORE were extended universally through
the British isles, we should soon have little
cause to complain of asperity and hostility
among our Christian brethren. When once
the various denominations of Christians shall
be taught by our example, to add to godliness
loving kindness,—and to loving kindness,
charity,—their minds will be prepared to admire
the excellence of the church establishment,
and duly to appreciate its tendency to promote
every moral virtue. The heart, which will not
yield to the vehemence of argument, may be
softened by kindness and forbearance ; and the
most cold and obdurate prejudices may be

* Observations on Report, No. CXLII.

melted down by the warmth of Christian love
and charity.

When I see the doughty champions of any
sect, drawn up in martial array, and engaged
in the hostility of wordy argument,—deeply
conversant in all the tactics of the church
militant, and directing the canon of their establishment against those who differ from them
only in points, as to which revelation hath not
explicitly and distinctly declared the divine
will, and about which Christians who refer to
the Scripture as the only unerring rule, and
agree in all essential points, may yet con-
scientiously differ,—I hold them to be defective in true policy, as well as in genuine Christianity; and I venture to apply the words of
OUR BLESSED LORD, and to say, " Ye know
" not what spirit ye are of."—While the
breach between sincere and honest believers is
thus increased, our pure and undefiled religion
is injured and deformed ; and the very cause,
in behalf of which hostilities are waged, is injured and deteriorated. These are not the
means, by which the interests of genuine Christianity are to be promoted ;—this is not the
way in which the English church, that pure
and reformed part of it to which we have the

happiness to belong, is to be defended against
its open and concealed enemies.

> Love and meekness
> Become a christian better than ambition.
> Win straying souls with modesty again;
> Cast none away.—

He who induces me to extend my interest
and my affections, to other climates, and to
other states,—to different sects, opinions, and
classes of men,—who enlarges the circle of my
benevolence,—who instructs me that we are all
children of our heavenly Father, all united by
one common sympathy, all subject to the same
trials and afflictions, and all inheritors of the
same blessed hopes,—He is my kindest and my
best friend:—He is the friend and benefactor
of mankind.

These are principles conducive to the happiness of all mankind; they are applicable to all
nations, and to all ages. But if ever there was
a period, if ever there was a country, in which
the practical adoption of them was an essential
act of political wisdom,—if ever there was a
subject to which they were peculiarly applicable, it is to the present state of our sister
island. It is upon the wisdom or folly, the
justice or injustice, of our proceedings,—upon

the Christian or anti-christian spirit of our counsels,—that will depend the secure preservation of Ireland, as a blessing to us,—or its precarious possession, as a thorn in the sides of Britain.

The late application from some Roman Catholics of affluence and rank in Ireland, called upon many statesmen, and among others upon our respected President to declare his sentiments freely and unreservedly, in the Upper House of Parliament.—To all of *toleration*, that could be asked, he was a friend : but he objected to the *demand of power*. He wished that something had been applied for, in which the general mass of Irish Catholics was concerned;—something that was connected with personal toleration;—something that was to promote the social and domestic habits of the labouring class, or to improve their resources ; —something that was to have a general operation in bettering the condition of our Catholic fellow subjects in Ireland. But as to granting to Papists the power of sitting in Parliament, of exercising corporate franchises, and of acting as Sheriffs of counties,—he called upon the noble Lords to pause, until they had ascertained, whether such after concessions, we should be able to

obtain toleration for our Protestant fellow subjects in Ireland ; and whether we should be able
to keep inviolate the barriers of our religious
and political communion, and to preserve that
entire, which can only be preserved by its en-
tirety.

We shall proceed with an extract from that
part of BISHOP BARRINGTON's speech on this
occasion, which is peculiarly applicable to this
subject. " After a period," says his Lordship,
" of religious difference and civil discord, it is
" indeed of the utmost importance, that we
" should be influenced by an increased anxiety,
" to guard against every unfair or unfavour-
" able impression, from recent injuries, or from
" internal discontents. It is essential that we
" should resolve to preserve inviolate and
" sacred the principles of the establishment;
" and to extend that toleration, forbearance,
" and Christian charity, which are its distinc-
" tive marks, to their utmost practical limit.—
" RELIGIOUS TOLERATION is the primary
" principle, and peculiar characteristic, of our
" established church. By the practice of it,
" we have been habituated to respect and revere
" even the errors of the conscientious Chris-

" tian; and we have been able to preserve
" harmony and good will, not only between
" Protestant sects, but between every denomi
" nation of Christians."

" How far it is the disposition of the English
" to shew, not merely toleration, but real and
" and active beneficence, to persons differing
" from them in articles of faith, may have ap-
" peared by the reception and protection which
" this country has recently afforded to the
" French priests:—where to religious preju-
" dices was superadded political danger; and
" when we had no security against the intro-
" duction of spies and enemies; nor any rea-
" sonable assurance that there might not be
" individuals among them, desirous of pur-
" chasing their return, on almost any condi-
" tions, which the usurped power of the French
" government might think proper to dictate."

" In that instance we had also to encounter
" religious danger, from that bigoted spirit of
" conversion, which characterises their reli-
" gion;—from the unfavourable sentiments
" which they had nourished from their in-
" fancy, with respect to English protestants;
" —and from a peculiar species of domineering
" intolerance, which distinguishes the French

" from all other nations.—And yet these con-
" siderations did not deter us from receiving
" them with all the warm charity of Christians,
" and with all the liberality of Englishmen ;
" —exhibited not merely by the higher orders
" in the hour of plenty, but by the poor and
" necessitous at a period of general scarcity."

" In looking to the welfare of the great mass
" of Roman Catholics in Ireland, I mean that
" useful body of men which in every coun-
" try must compose the most numerous class of
" its inhabitants, it will be wise and benevolent
" so to use the power which the constitution
" has placed in us, as a part of a Protestant
" legislature, as to do for them, individually,
" all that (were the power in their hands) they
" would be wise in doing for themselves. In
" this view it may be a subject for our consi-
" deration, how we can better provide for the
" discharge of their religious duties, and to
" what degree we may with propriety assist
" them in that respect. We may inquire
" how far we can improve their temporal con-
" dition by supplying the means and motives
" of industry, and by every exertion of kind-
" ness, which can promote their domestic com-
" fort, improve their character, and meliorate

" their condition :—and we may endeavour to
" make a more general provision for the edu-
" cation of their children ; not interfering with
" their religious tenets,—but attending to their
" instruction and to making them useful to
" themselves and to the community, and giving
" them the unequivocal advantage of religious
" and moral habits."—

When* we contemplate the great number of
children of the Irish poor who are totally neglected as to their education, it must be apparent
that there has been something defective in point
of true policy. It should seem that every
Kingdom is capable of educating its own children ; and that to do that, is not only a duty,
but an essential act of wisdom in the state.
Much, it is to be acknowledged, has been
attempted in Ireland, both by government
and by individuals ; but a general system of
education, and a radical improvement in the
moral character of the lower orders in Ireland,
cannot be expected from the energy of the poor
themselves, nor yet from the benevolence of
individuals, nor even from *occasional and un-
connected* acts of government. It requires a
general, an arranged, a powerful system of

* Observations on Report, No. CXVII.

measures; calculated to conciliate the good will of all sects; and (to quote their own words) " such as would satisfy our brethren of every " other persuasion, that the object is, not to " proselyte individuals who entertain senti- " ments different from our own, but to establish " the conviction of those important truths, " which are held in common by every descrip- " tion of Christians."

It must, indeed, be evident to the most superficial observer, that the formation and execution of any plan for the desired and neces- sary melioration of the condition and character of the lower classes of the community in Ire- land, will require a greater degree of strength, more arrangement of system, and more con- tinuance of action, than can ever be expected from any efforts, or even from any union or co-operation, of individuals in that country. It will not be less obvious, that such a plan will require a more fixed and unbroken attention, and will occupy a greater portion of time in the detail, than can possibly be supplied by ministers, who are already fully engaged with the other momentous concerns of a great and extended empire.

Those who have had means of communication with the gentlemen most active in the late measures for the benefit of the Irish poor, must have been again and again gratified by the warm and earnest attention, that has been paid to this subject by government, as well as by individuals. What has been doing by the Dublin Society,—by that for promoting the comforts of the poor,—by the association for discountenancing vice,—by the fever institutions, —in the Dublin House of Industry and Foundling Hospital,—at Cork, Waterford, Killaloe, New Ross, and other places, is certainly intitled to every degree of praise and commendation. But these institutions do little more than shew what is practicable; making part of a general system, and supplying the means and example of what is to be done. Measures must be adopted by government for awakening, in every part of Ireland, a spirit of improvement;—the objects of which may be classed under the three following heads:—

1st, The promotion of schools, generally and effectually extended to the children of all the poor in Ireland.—It may not be possible entirely to put out of the question the distinction of the sects, which are prevalent in that country: but, upon their own authority I may

be allowed to submit that EDUCATION, not
conversion, ought to be the object of these
schools ; and that they should be made as con-
tributory to industry and civilized happiness,
and as acceptable and inviting to all denominations of Christians, as may be done with any
degree of propriety and security.

2d. The providing of additional means and
motives to domestic employment and domestic
management in cottages ; so as not only to
meliorate individual character, but also to increase the amount and benefit of national industry.—The poor in some parts of Ireland
derive great advantage from their spinning-
wheels, and from the domestic occupation
which they supply : but those benefits are not
universally extended; and it may be doubted
whether they ever will be. In the Reports of
the Society (No. CVI), the reader will find an
account of the late introduction of the manufacture of split straw into this country, and of
the effects which it has produced in some of our
parishes. It will appear from that, and from
a paper in the Appendix to the fourth volume,
that no difficulty or expense would attend the
introduction of it into the cottages in Ireland ;
and that it would afford the means of employ-

ing and educating a large proportion of those
children; that are at present unprovided for.
The raw material is very cheap, the work is
easily learnt, and requires very little exertion ;
at the same that it is friendly to *personal cleanliness* and to domestic habits.

3d. The general extension of fever institutions, vaccination, and of other charities for
preserving the poor from the ravages of infectious disorders, and the conducting of them in
such a manner, as to produce a favourable impression on the minds of the poor, and to increase
the communication between them and the rich,
and thereby accustom them to look to the other
classes for kindness and assistance. This would
be deserving of all the attention that could be
applied to those desirable objects.

Though Ireland has the advantage of being
unincumbered with our system of poor laws, and
though the Irish have a degree of activity and
fervour of mind which we are not so fortunate
as to possess in England, yet it must be repeated
that there are many circumstances, which render
it impossible that the great and necessary improvements in the condition of the poor in Ireland, should be produced by mere individual
exertion and co-operation. It is, however, essen-

tial that the efforts of individuals should go hand
in hand with any measures of government;
and that in the arrangement of those measures,
not merely *opinions*, but even *wishes* and *prejudices*, should be consulted ; so as to conciliate
the co-operation of as many persons *of all sects
and orders*, as may be practicable. Without
it, the best directed acts of government will be
incompetent to their object ; and with it, effectually obtained, there will be little required
but arrangement and direction of general plans,
and occasional aid thrown in, as seed, to be
abundantly repaid by productive industry, and
by melioration of character: for it would afford
evidence that the measures were defective, if
they had not the operation of increasing the
exertions of individuals in Ireland, and of
diminishing gradually and sensibly the calls on
the public fund for aid and support.

The proposal, therefore. for the consideration of those to whom alone it can be addressed,
is, that a BOARD be established, the members of
which shall be selected from those Irish Privy
Counsellors, who, by means of the official
situations which they hold or have held in Ireland, possess information as to the internal
situation and circumstances of the country.

This Board, it is submitted, should be open to proposals, suggestions, communications, and petitions, from every part of Ireland; upon which reports should be made to government, from time to time, as circumstances might require.

Instead of apprehending that private charities might be checked by such an establishment, one may venture to express a confidence, and that founded on experience, that the efforts and exertions of the land owners and gentlemen would be thereby increased and encouraged, in every part of Ireland; when they saw an office so established and sanctioned by government, expressly to pay attention to, and assist their endeavours to meliorate the character and condition of their tenants and neighbours. At present the difficulty is great, because the appearance is formidable. No one, however, doubts the expediency of improvements, in the morals and industry of the country, where they have property or are resident. And be it remembered, where labour is made easy and pleasurable, and examples of success are frequent, exertion and co-operation will never be wanting in the cause of humanity.

I admit that the preparing and arranging of

plans for the improvement of the Irish poor, will require a considerable degree of steady and continued attention on the part of one or two of the committee. The attendance, however, of the other members may be on the same footing as that of the Board of Agriculture, or of the Society for bettering the condition of the poor. The situation may be made honourable and respectable, and the labour chiefly confined to the first proceedings and arrangements; the duty being to advise and report, but not to decide and carry into execution. It would therefore be perfectly unnecessary that there should be any salary for the members of the Board; and the expense of the whole establishment, might be so trifling, as not to exceed *five hundred pounds* a year.

The present moment does not indeed at first view, appear to be open to new projects, and new suggestions of civil improvements. It will appear, however, that there are circumstances peculiarly favourable to a measure of this kind at present. The necessity of some melioration of character and condition in the poor of Ireland, is become so pressing and imperious, as to be felt by every one. A crisis of public danger and calamity has been always found to soften, prepare, and awaken the human mind, and to produce the most favourable disposition for improvement, exertion, and co-operation :— and the personal characters of the leading men in Ireland, as well as in England, are such, as to offer advantages in the commencement of so arduous and important an undertaking.

The influence * of the school establishment of Scotland on the peasantry of that country, seems to have decided (if evidence were yet wanting) the important question—whether a system of national instruction for the poor be favorable to morals and good government.   In the year 1698, Fletcher of Saltoun declared as follows : " There are at this day, in Scot-
" land, two hundred thousand people begging
" from door to door.   And though the number
" of them be perhaps double to what it was for-
" merly, by reason of this present great distress,
" *(a famine then prevailed)* yet in all times there
" have been about one hundred thousand of
" those vagabonds, who have lived without
" any regard or subjection either to the laws of
" the land, or even those of God and nature ;
" fathers incestuously accompanying with their

* Observations on Report No. CXXVIII, by the late Dr Currie,

" own daughters, the son with the mother, and
" the brother with the sister." He goes on to
say, that no magistrate could discover that
they had ever been baptized, or in what way
one in a hundred went out of the world. He
accuses them as frequently guilty of robbery,
and sometimes of murder: " In years of
" plenty," says he, " many thousands of them
" meet together in the mountains ; where they
" feast and riot for many days : and at country
" weddings, markets, burials, and other public
" occasions, they are to be seen, both men and
" women, perpetually drunk ; cursing, blas-
" pheming, and fighting together."* This
high minded statesman, of whom it is said by a
contemporary, " that he would lose his life
" readily to save his country, and would not
" do a base thing to serve it," thought the evil
so great, that he proposed as a remedy the
revival of domestic slavery, according to the
practice of his adored republics in the classic
ages. A better remedy has been found, which
in the silent lapse of a century has proved
effectual. The statute of 1696, the noble legacy
of the Scottish parliament to their country,

* Political Works of Andrew Fletcher; 8vo. London,
1737, p. 144.

began soon after this to operate ; and happily as the minds of the poor received instruction, the Union opened new channels of industry, and new fields of action to their view.

At the present day there is perhaps no country in Europe, in which, in proportion to its population,* so small a number of crimes fall under the chastisement of the criminal law, as Scotland. We have the best authority for asserting that on an average of thirty years, preceding the year 1797, the executions in that division of the island † did not amount to six

* It may appear fanciful to mention among the causes of the melioration of the Scotch character, their instruction in Music, so as not only to introduce Psalms and Hymns in divine service, but at social meetings ; a circumstance, which, with pleasure, I remember in the early part of my life in New England, and which I have had great satisfaction in witnessing during the preceding summer in Scotland. It is not a small advantage, to beguile the weary moments of solitary labour, or to fill up the pause of social intercourse, with Psalms, Hymns, and cheerful Songs. " Music" (says the venerable Hooker) " delighteth all ages, and beseemeth all " states;—as seasonable in grief as in joy;—as decent, being " added unto actions of greatest weight and solemnity, as being " used when men most sequester themselves from action."

† That Scotland, notwithstanding the general introduction of *Cotton Mills and other Manufactures* into that part of our island, still possesses the same honourable superiority, will will appear from the following extract from the speech of the Lord Chief Justice Clerk, at the conclusion of the circuit, at Glasgow, on Friday the 29th of April, 1808.—" It

annually; and one quarter sessions, for the
town of Manchester only, has sent, according

" may be said that commerce and manufactures hardly existed
" in this country during the earlier period of the last century.
" —True, but now, at least in those respects, we are treading
" fast on the heels of England, and yet, thank God, the same
" consequences do not follow.   In this very city and district
" where I now sit, commerce and manufactures of all kinds
" have been long introduced to an extent, equal to any place
" or district of the kingdom, the capital alone excepted—and
" yet it was stated by a political writer, but a few years ago,
" that one Quarter Sessions at Manchester, sends more
" criminals to transportation than all Scotland in a year.—
" We must, therefore, look to other causes for the good order
" and morality of our people, and I think we have not far to
" look.   In my opinion, that cause is to be found chiefly *in*
" *our institutions for the education of youth,* and for the main-
" tenance of religion,—The institution of PAROCHIAL
" SCHOOLS, in the manner and to the extent in which
" they are established in Scotland, is, I believe, peculiar to
" ourselves; and it is an institution, to which, however simple
" in its nature and unobtrusive in its operation, I am per-
" suaded we are chiefly to ascribe the regularity of conduct
" by which we are distinguished.—The child of the meanest
" peasant, of the lowest mechanic in this country, may (and
" most of them do) receive a virtuous education from their
" earliest youth.   At our parochial schools, they are not
" only early initiated in the principles of our holy religion and
" in the soundest doctrines of morality, but most of them re-
" ceive different degrees of education in other respects, which
" qualify them to earn their bread in life in various ways, and
" which, independent even of religious instruction, by enlarg-
" ing the understanding, necessarily raise a man in his own
" estimation, and set him above the mean and dirty crimes,
" to which the temptations and hardships of life might other-
" wise expose him."

to Mr. Hume, more felons to the plantations than all the judges of Scotland usually do in the space of a year.* It might appear invidious to attempt a calculation of the many thousand individuals in Manchester, and its vicinity, who can neither read nor write. A majority of those who suffer the punishment of death for their crimes in every part of England, are, it is believed, in this miserable state of ignorance.

There is now a legal provision for parochial schools, or rather for a school in each of the different townships into which the country is divided, in several of the northern states of North America. They are, however, of recent origin there, excepting in New England, where they were established in the last century,† probably about the same time as in Scotland, and by the same religious sect. In the Protestant cantons of Switzerland, the peasantry have the advantage of similar schools, though established and endowed in a different manner. This is also the case in certain districts in England, particularly in the northern parts of Yorkshire

* Hume's Commentaries on the Laws of Scotland, Introduction, p. 50.

† The act for the support of FREE SCHOOLS in the province of Massachusets Bay, was passed in 1692. A copy of it is inserted in the latter part of this volume.

and of Lancashire, and in the counties of Westmorland and Cumberland.

A law, providing for the instruction of the poor, was passed by the parliament of Ireland ; but the fund has been diverted from its purpose, and the measure entirely frustrated.

The similarity of character between the Swiss, and the Scotch, and the people of New England, can scarcely be overlooked. That it arises in a great measure from the similarity of their institutions for instruction, cannot be questioned. It is no doubt increased by physical causes. With a superior degree of instruction, each of these nations possesses a country that may be said to be sterile, in the neighbourhood of countries comparatively rich. Hence emigrations, and the other effects on conduct and character, which such circumstances naturally produce. This subject is in a high degree curious. The points of dissimilarity between these nations might be traced to their causes also ; and the whole investigation would perhaps admit of an approach to certainty in our conclusions, to which such inquiries seldom lead. How much superior in morals, in intellect, and in happiness, the peasantry of those parts of England, are which have opportunities of instruction, to the same class in other situations, those who inquire into the subject will speedily discover. The peasantry of Westmorland, and of the other districts mentioned above, if their physical and moral qualities be taken together, appear to possess a considerable degree of superiority over the peasantry of any part of the island.

A system * of moral and religious instruction, *connecting the rising generation with our civil and ecclesiastical establishment,* will therefore be found to be not only the first act of charity † but the wisest measure of the state. At the present awful crisis of the world, it is

---

* See the Introductory Letter to the fourth volume of the Reports.

† Of all the means of soothing the distresses, improving the habits, and encouraging the virtues, of the poor, none will be found more gratifying, or more effectual, than a general and impartial provision for the EDUCATION of their children.— The affection and the interest of the parent is ever, through the boundless variety of creation, increased with the necessity of the offspring. The cottager, hopeless of elevation himself, looks with desire and anxiety to the prosperity of his child : and where, by the influence of education, extended to every class of life,—talent, industry, and prudence, are enabled to rise in the world,—the weakest and most prejudiced eye will see the use of the gradations of rank and wealth ; and will be sensible of their beneficial effects, in stimulating the activity and industry of the individual, and thereby infusing health, vigour, and vital strength, into the body politic.

of increased and accumulated consequence; as the hope and expectation of the country will, in a great degree, depend upon its effect and influence.—Whether we regard, generally, the fallen state of man, and the consequent corruption of our nature,—or, directing our view to the British empire, we estimate the recent and unmeasured increase of wealth, luxury, and dissipation in this country,—or whether we turn our eyes to Europe and contemplate the seeds of anarchy, insubordination, and infidelity, so industriously and so successfully disseminated over the modern world,—we shall discover causes of civil disorder and dissolution, which must appall the most undaunted mind. We all are sensible that the present and immediate palliative is the firm and provident administration of the means of government: but the true *medicine of the soul*,—the restorative to health and strength,—the only effectual and unfailing remedy *for the moral evils of civil society*,—is a general system of religious and virtuous education.

Whatever prejudices may have existed on this subject in monkish ages, they are happily, and I trust for ever removed.—No pious Christian, no loyal subject, now objects to that instruction, which fits and prepares the individual to thrive, and to be useful, in his appropriate situation of life,—which instructs him in the superior advantages of civil liberty, and of permanent government;—and, at the same time that it shews him his duty here, directs his views to another state of existence hereafter, and explains to him, from holy writ, the fallen state of man, and the appointed means of salvation. by the atonement and intercession of a Redeemer.

The superior advantages of such instruction, have been felt and proved, wherever the experiment has been tried. Its effects in part of Somersetshire, in schools established and supported by the Christian benevolence of two individuals, and by the meek and unassuming piety of one * who is now gone to receive her reward, have been already stated in these Reports. In Westmorland, in Scotland, in America, and Switzerland, if we may correctly estimate by the example of persons who have

* The pious and excellent Mrs. HOCKER, of Weston, near Bath. An account of her schools, which was given in the Reports, No. XCVII, will be found in a subsequent part of this volume ; as also of those of Miss H. MORE, and Miss P. MORE, which are to be found, No. LXIV, in the Reports of the Society.

fixed in our metropolis, it has been attended
with two invaluable benefits :—one, the abstinence from that practice, so destructive to the
English and Irish poor,—the intemperate use
of spirituous liquors ;—the other, an extraordinary exemption from criminal habits,—a circumstance known, and observed on, by almost
every court of justice, not only in the British
isles, but in Europe.

England is fortunate in the liberal endowment of a numerous variety of charity schools,*
which do honour to the country. But it would
be blindness not to perceive, that though they
may have had some effect in preserving the
moral habits of many of the poor, yet in
many places they are not entirely adequate to
their object, and in others the poor receive
very little, if any advantage from them. Instances might be referred to, in which a single
scholar forms the whole population of a well

* LORD KENYON has observed very justly, that if those who
have the superintendance or controul over schools had done
their duty, we should not find, as is now the case, *empty walls
without scholars*, and every thing neglected but the receipt of
the salaries and emoluments. IN SOME INSTANCES (he adds)
THAT HAVE LATELY COME WITHIN MY OWN KNOW-
LEDGE, THERE WAS NOT A SINGLE SCHOLAR IN THE
SCHOOLS, THOUGH THERE WERE VERY LARGE ENDOW-
MENTS TO THEM.—*The King and the Archbishop of York.*
Michaelmas 1795.

endowed charity school. In some, the master
and usher receive their respective salaries and
advantages, without even the incumbrance of a
single pupil; and in no part of England, (with
exception to a wise and benevolent plan now
executing by the Bishop of Durham in his
diocese) has any arrangement been formed, or
effort made, *to extend generally to all the poor* *
the benefits of a religious and moral education.—The annual display indeed of charity
children in the metropolis, is splendid and im-
pressive. But if it were known, how small is
our comparative provision for education; the
total amount of these scholars would be less
a matter of exultation, than the thousands of
poor children, who at present receive no benefit
whatever from our public charity schools, would

---

* Upon reference to the written laws of the different parts
of the empire, we shall find the *Irish* statutes from the 28th
of Henry VIII. to the present period, supplying a series of acts
in favour of education in *Ireland*. In *Scotland*, one of their
latest statutes, before the Union, made a provision for *free
schools in every parish* in that kingdom; and one of our early
acts, after the Union, supplied the sum of 20,000*l.* for the
establishment of schools in the *Highlands.*—In the *English Statute Book*, however, from the reign of Queen Elizabeth,
to the present day, no notice occurs of schools and schoolmasters, nor any reference to education *in England*, except
by *restrictions on schoolmasters;* imposing *disabilities and in
capacities*, instead of providing *support and encouragement.*

be matter of deep regret to the philanthropic observer.

Some individuals have entertained an apprehension, that it is possible that the prevalence of other schools than those of our own persuasion,* and the zeal and activity of the conductors of those schools, may produce, on the rising generation, effects unfavourable to our national and established church.   If it should

This case has come within my own observation,—where a parent zealously attached to the doctrines and ritual of the established church, and having long waited for her child's admission into the parochial school, has at length accepted the offer of admission into a Methodist school; preferring the benefit of a Christian education there, to the continuance of an hopeless application to her own church.— If I should be asked how it would be practicable to extend, at a small expense, the means of education to *all the children of the poor*, I should refer a subsequent part of this volume, and to THE SCHOOLS IN WEST STREET.—If the charity and other schools in England were opened to all the poor, on the same weekly allowance, as is regularly paid by the poor in that instance (presuming the master's duty to be properly performed) there would be very few of the poor, whose moral and religious improvement would be neglected.   In cases where extreme poverty hath made the parent an object of parish relief, I can see no more objection to the magistrate being authorized to direct the weekly payment of three-pence each for children, between the ages of nine and twelve years, towards their *education*, and the improvement of their *morals, industry*, and *religions habits*, than to his having the power of granting six times the sum towards their *mere animal subsistence.*

appear to temperate men, that such an apprehension is not entirely groundless, the consequences will be too important to be neglected: and the causes will appear to be too deeply founded in real and existing circumstances, to admit of any other prevention, except what I trust all our Christian brethren will rejoice in, —*the adoption, on our part, of the same extended and general system of* EDUCATION, *regulated according to the rites and doctrines of the Church of England.* Whoever, indeed, is anxious for the duration and prosperity of our establishment, whether in church or in state, must be interested in the adoption of a prudent and practicable extension of the means of education;—so that its benefits may be offered to every individual; as a preservative, not only for youth, but for the other ages of the poor, against the taint of sedition, and the poison of infidelity.

ACCOUNTS OF SCHOOLS

CHIEFLY EXTRACTED

FROM THE

REPORTS OF THE SOCIETY;

WITH OTHER PAPERS,

ON THE SUBJECT OF THE

EDUCATION OF THE POOR.

No. I.

DAY SCHOOLS AT BOLDRE.

THE two schools at Boldre,* in the New
Forest, were established and opened on the first
of July, 1791, by the Rev. Mr. Gilpin; one
for twenty boys, the other for twenty girls, to
be selected from the children of the day-labour-
ing poor of the parish; a preference being given
(in order to encourage reading) to children
who have learnt to read a chapter in the Testament: but, if the prescribed number of such
scholars cannot be found, the deficiency is supplied by such children as cannot read.

Sixty-three boys and fifty nine girls have
already been admitted, including those at present in the schools. Their attendance com-
mences at nine o'clock, when all the scholars
are assembled for prayers. From twelve to
one is allowed for dinner, which the children
bring with them to school; they are dismissed
in summer at five, and in winter at four o'clock;

* Reports, No. XXXV.

except on Saturdays, when the school breaks up at twelve. If any one is absent, or is beyond the fixed time, without a proper excuse, such child is punished by an hour's confinement and employment, at noon in winter, and in the evening in summer: and if the children were to be kept at home, so as to continue absent without leave (which leave is to be entered in a book for inspection of the visitors) they would be dismissed the school, and their places filled up by such as would attend and make a better use of their time. As to vacation, a week is allowed at Whitsuntide, a fortnight at Christmas, and a month at harvest, in order to give them an opportunity of benefiting by harvest work.

The girls are taught to read, knit, spin, sew, and mend their own clothes, so as to fit them to be useful daughters, and good wives; the boys (besides being improved in their reading) are instructed in writing and arithmetic; in the first, so far as to write a legible hand, for which one copy a day is thought sufficient: and in arithmetic, so far as the four first rules, and particularly in the tables that belong to those rules.

No precise time is fixed for admission; in

order that the children in the parish may be
encouraged to an early proficiency in reading,
as the qualification for a place in the school:
nor is any precise time fixed for the removal
of either the boys or girls; as it is presumed
that as soon as they are made *really useful,*
their parents will wish to take them away, and
thereby room will be left for the admission of
other children. They usually come from seven
to nine years of age, and quit the school at
thirteen or fourteen. As an incitement to industry, a separate account is kept of the produce of each girl's sale work; and such produce is laid out for them, in clothes and neces-
saries, at the end of the year. Petty offences
are punished by a little extra confinement in
play hours; but no corporal correction is allowed, except for lying, swearing, stealing, in-
decent language, or immorality.

At the end of November, the annual account
of the work of the girls is made up; and, from
thence to Christmas, their working hours are
employed, *gratis,* in making up shirts and shifts
for the children in the school, and in knitting
stockings (a pair each for the boys and girls)
the worsted for which is given them.—At the
end of the year, all the children attend at the

vicarage; where their clothes are examined: if there has been neglect on their part, it is noticed: and additions are, at the same time, made to their clothing.

The great object of the founder of these schools is to promote in these children the *knowledge and practice* of religion; in order that they may be able therein to instruct their own children, when they have families; an instruction, that, from local circumstances, is much wanted in the neighbourhood of the New Forest. For this purpose, Mr. Gilpin has drawn up an easy explanation of the duties of religion,* by way of question and answer. This the children are taught to repeat, as well as their catechism, and are examined in it on Tuesday and Friday after dinner, and on Sunday afternoon.

In the course of a visit to-day at the schools, I had the pleasure of observing the progress of the boys in arithmetic and writing, of the girls

---

* This explanation of the duties of religion would be a very useful book in all parochial schools. Mr. Gilpin has complied with a request of having a cheap edition of it sold by Messrs. Cadell and Davies, in the Strand. I trust it will prove of great service, in opening and improving the minds of parish children, by religious and moral instruction. *B.*

30th *April*, 1798.

in reading and work, and of all of them in decency and propriety of deportment. I heard part of Mr. Gilpin's explanation of the duties of religion read in the school; and was extremely struck with their attention, and apparent intelligence as to what was read. The manner contributed to fix the sense in their minds: the mistress first reads the question; and then each girl, in turn, the answer; and I am much deceived by appearances, and extremely mistaken in my conjectures, if the religious instruction, which they are now receiving at an early age, is not so fixed and imprinted in their minds, as to remain a permanent blessing to the latest hour of their lives, and to descend as an hereditary benefit to their children.

The annual expense of this useful establishment does not exceed forty guineas a year. The master, who lives in the house, has for salary and finding fuel, &c. 21*l.* a year, and the habitation and garden. The mistress lives in the village; she has ten guineas a year: and Mr. Gilpin's donations of clothing to the children: and some other incidental expenses, amount to nearly ten guineas a year more.

The school house is a neat brick building,

with the boys' school at the end next the road ; and, at the other the dwelling house, comprizing the school of the girls, and looking into the garden. It is built on a healthy and beautiful situation, with a gradual descent to Lymington river. It cost 210*l*. On the walls of the school room are various texts of Scripture inscribed in tablets. The children stand round the table at particular times, and read them over, with a view of imprinting on their memory some of the most useful precepts in the Testament.

For the permament endowment of these schools after his death, Mr. Gilpin proposes to provide by the sale of his Drawings and Sketches, which, when I was there, he had formed for that purpose into eighty-nine lots, each lot containing several Drawings. How valuable an addition they will make to the collection of the artist, the connoisseur, and the lover of the fine arts, it will be unnecessary and presumptuous in me to endeavour to explain. The value of the Drawings, enhanced by the object to which the produce is destined to be applied, must render them an enviable possession to every one, whenever (in consequence of that event, which the friends of humanity hope

may be long delayed) they shall be offered to
the public.

The benefit of such schools, as those founded
by Mr. Gilpin, at Boldre, is important in every
situation, and at all times ; but, in the New
Forest, where the children of the poor have too
much disposition to partake of the natural wild-
ness of the place, they are peculiarly necessary
and beneficial.—In point of justice, it is due to
the poor of Boldre to observe, that they are very
sensible of its utility, and very desirous that
their children may participate of the benefit of it.
The requisite qualification of some progress in
reading, has contributed to a general advancement of learning and civilization in the parish,
and (which is of great use) to the support of
several little schools there for the first rudiments of instruction.—I have only to add my
earnest wish, that these schools may long
flourish, according to the benevolent will of
the founder; and that his example may produce many imitators, in every part of the
kingdom.

5*th April,* 1798.

No. II.

MENDIP DAY SCHOOLS AT CHEDDAR, &c.

THE Mendip schools* are situate in the part
of Somersetshire, between Wells, Bristol, and
the channel which divides Wales from England. They extend over twelve parishes, which
are dispersed throughout a district of country,
about twenty-five miles in diameter. They
are intended not merely for the education of
youth, but for the instruction and reformation
of mature life, and for the improvement and
consolation of the aged ; and, according to the
circumstances of each parish, are opened daily,
or twice or thrice a week, or on Sundays only.
The early part of the Sabbath is devoted to the
instruction of the young, who afterwards proceed to church in a body, to attend divine service. Towards the close of the day the room
is frequented by others; chiefly by the aged,
who come to take the benefit of the evening
readings and discourse, and attend with great
pleasure and eagerness, to derive from religious

information and society that solid relief, which alone can give comfort to declining life, and smooth the path to their grave. Their stay in the school is for half an hour, an hour, or more, as their convenience or inclination directs. The number of those who frequent the schools, including children and parents, is about three thousand.

Ten years ago that neighbourhood exhibited a very different appearance. There are few gentlemen's seats; scarcely any resident clergy; and there was little to be seen in that country which could distinguish it as in civilized society, or within the pale of Christianity. In the populous and extensive parish of Cheddar, the congregation at the parish church on an average did not exceed the number of *twenty*: —the regular attendants at that church are now *eight hundred*, and sometimes more. The precepts of Christianity were almost unknown and disregarded in that district:—they are now the comfort of the aged, and the guide of the young ; and the contemplation and observance of them have been attended by a rich and abundant harvest of moral virtues ;—of honesty, sobriety, diligence, industry, and chastity.

All this has been effected by the labour of

two individuals, who, fortunately for this country, fixed their residence there, about ten years ago.—As the means of relieving and assisting their uninstructed neighbours, they hired an house at Cheddar, one of the twelve parishes, and in this they established a school; they engaged for it an intelligent master and mistress, and opened the doors, not only to uneducated children, but to all the poor of the parish. The young were allowed to attend for instruction during an hour or two, or such other time as their daily labour, or ordinary occupations of life, permitted. On the Lord's day the house was opened as a Sunday school: and in the evening of that day a Sunday aged society, the first example of the kind; where the two patronesses of the school were present, read a sermon, and conversed with the old people who attended.

When such benefit and satisfaction were attainable, it is no wonder that, in despight of ignorance and prejudice, and of every opposition which they could make, the scholars became more numerous, and the audience increased. The schools were extended to other places: and in the poorer parishes female societies, under the direction of the two patronesses and of two female stewards, were formed for the relief of poor women on the following plan:—that each member should pay one shilling entrance, and three halfpence a week, to be paid on the second Monday in the month; but subject to forfeiture, on neglect of payment for three succeeding months;—in case of sickness, each member to be allowed three shillings and sixpence a week for four weeks, and afterwards one shilling and sixpence a week until they recover;—in case of death, the fund to contribute one guinea, and each member sixpence to the funeral; and in case of child-birth, every married woman to be allowed seven shillings and sixpence at her lying-in, in case she has been married nine months. No member is admissible under the age of fourteen, or above the age of forty-five, or in an infirm state of health; or to be entitled to any contribution, until after she has been a member twelve months. In case of a call for relief, application is to be made to one of the stewards, whose duty it is to visit the party, and examine, and report upon the case.

After several regulations to prevent and punish impropriety of conduct or discourse, and to provide for the continuance of the society, it is declared that the annual meeting shall be in the beginning of July, when the patronesses, stewards, and members, shall attend divine service, and a sermon ; and to save the club all expenses incident to such annual meetings, and to prevent the necessity of women being seen at a public house, the entertainment is at the cost of the patronesses, who engage to treat the company with tea and cakes, so long as they continue to behave themselves well, and are punctual in sending their children to school. In order to encourage chastity and good morals in the single women, the patronesses present every young woman of *good character*, who has been educated in their schools, and continues to attend religious instruction there, with five shillings, a new Bible, and a pair of white stockings, on the day of marriage.*

In the course of four years, from October, 1789, the time of the commencement of the first of these schools, a very considerable progress was made ; the education of youth had

* This is abridged from the " Articles of Agreement to be " observed by a Society of Women, held in the parishes of " Shipham and Rowbonow, in Somersetshire; commencing " in September, 1792." The reader would do well to apply for a copy of the rules at length.

been attended to, and the improvement and religious habits of the poor of every period of life, had been increased. The founders of these schools have not been unaware how essential and indispensable it is that the basis of all amendment and reformation in the poor, (and the principle applies equally to the rich) should be laid in religion, and in christian knowledge. Until the scholar is impressed with a deep sense of the fallen state of man, and of the corruption of human nature, no effectual and permanent reform can be produced in the human heart; nor can any warning be profitably given against idleness, drunkenness, or dishonesty, until the mind is subjected to the influence of Christianity, and supplied with religious motives of conduct, so as to fill up the vacancy of idle and vicious amusements. Without it the best resolutions of man are fickle and uncertain, existing only till a more potent influence shall be exerted against them.

The reader will have observed that, to promote sobriety and decency of habit in these female societies, all the social meetings are held at the school house, and the entertainments, consisting of cakes and tea, are at the expense of the patronesses; and that, in order to give a value to chastity, the basis of almost every other female virtue, rewards, consisting of a small sum of money, a large Bible, and a pair of stockings knit by one of the donors, are bestowed by these two ladies upon the marriage of every scholar of good character. They are delivered publicly, and with solemnity; and though of not much apparent value, are deemed very great objects of attainment.

The anniversary meeting of these societies and schools is generally early in July. Of that held on the 8th day of last August, I can give an account, from the relation of my Sister, Mrs. White, who was one of the ladies then present. The day begins with a breakfast at Miss H. More's house, at Cowslip Green, which is attended by the neighbouring families. From thence they adjourned to Shipham, one of their school houses, which was decorated by the hands of the children with wreaths and chaplets of natural flowers; every room, and the outside of the cottage, being white washed, and made a pattern of rural neatness. The company was invited to partake of a collation above stairs, while the better sort of poor were collecting together below to walk to the church in a procession, which was composed first of the school children of this and the adjoining parish, in number about one hundred and twenty, with their school mistresses; after them the clergyman, who was to preach, the vicar of the parish, and some of the neighbouring clergy, two and two. Then followed Miss Martha More, one of the patronesses, and her sister Mrs. More, of Bath, and the ladies, who were members of the society; followed by the poor who were members, and then the ladies and gentlemen who were introduced by members.

After divine service we had a discourse, exhorting the audience to fulfil all the duties of Christianity, in every rank and condition of society, and to set the example of a virtuous and religious life. The company then returned to the school, where the children were called over; each being noticed in its turn, and receiving the present of a plumb cake, with a particular commendation of every one who had been distinguished for good behaviour. The children were then dismissed; and the poor women, and some of the lesser farmers' wives and daughters, sat down to their entertainment of tea and cakes. The ladies assisted to make the tea, and butter the cakes; and in the course of an hour, in three rooms, about an hundred persons were served with attention and satisfaction. The yearly account of the society was then examined by Miss Martha More, with the assistance of the vicar, and his wife ; all the particulars were minutely explained to the members, and the balance in hand, amounting to rather better than 50*l.* was produced, as their fund for sickness or misfortune. It was stated that 50*l.* more had, with consent, been lent in the preceding year on government security ; which the poor expressed a wish it might be continued.—After the ladies and gentlemen present had tendered their benefactions to the society, and some members had been admitted whose character and conduct had been previously inquired into, and others entered, and their names referred for inquiry, the patronesses' wedding present, with some profitable advice, was given to a young woman, who had been married since the last meeting.

Miss Martha More then addressed herself to her poorer friends, with much energy and effect ;—to mothers, on good order in their families; on decency of conduct, and the efficacy of example : to young wives, on industry, attention, neatness, gentleness of manners, and good

temper : to young women, preparing for, or
going into service, on obedience, simplicity of
dress, and mutual kindness and affection to
each other.   She concluded with an animated
detail of the happy effects of a truly christian
spirit ; as supplying comfort during life, and
at the hour of death, and affording the hope of
eternal happiness hereafter.—The poor then
departed to their homes, having expressed their
gratitude, for the comforts they had derived
from the institution during the late severe winter, and having poured forth their earnest
wishes and prayers for the health of their absent
patroness, Miss Hannah More, who by severe
illness was prevented attending this anniversary meeting, which she had originally founded.

In giving this short and, I fear, imperfect
detail of what has been done for the benefit of
the poor and the ignorant, and for the promotion of true Christianity in the county of
Somerset, I do not presume to express an hope
that individuals will come forward in other
parts of England, who shall possess the abilities,
and will equal the active and persevering industry, of the founders of these schools.   They
have devoted the chief part of ten years to this
single and desirable object : an object, which

still continues to occupy almost all their attention and time.   Such exertions, and so great
sacrifices, are not to be expected from others;
nor are they necessary.   The example of what
has been done in this instance, may be adopted
upon a lower scale of energy and labour; it
may be applied to a single parish, or to a
small hamlet.   It may (without labour and
without a sacrifice of any of the rational pleasures or appropriate duties of life) become an
amusement, a gratification, and the means of
improvement, to every educated and independent person in every part of the kingdom.

No. III.

DAY SCHOOLS AT KENDAL.

In attempting to give an account of the schools*
which have been lately established for the education of poor children at Kendal, a populous manufacturing town in the county of
Westmorland, I must previously notice the
Blue Coat Schools, and the *Sunday Schools*,
which had existed in that place, prior to the introduction of that system of education, which
is peculiarly the subject of this paper. The
first of these schools, had been regularly visited
by the subscribers, and the children were
encouraged to attend the latter, and their parents to send them, by the prospect which has
been held out to both boys and girls, of being
elected into the *Blue Coat Schools*, or of obtaining the *green clothes*, which are the personal
donation of a charitable individual in that
place.—Still, however, there wanted system in
the arrangement of the plan ; and, in the execution, there was required the impulse of reward

---

* Reports, No. XC.

and encouragement, to occupy and command the attention of the children.

In May, 1797, Dr. Briggs submitted to the governors of the Sunday schools his sentiments on the subject of them. As those observations have produced a very beneficial effect at Kendal, and, with very few exceptions, will apply to *all the Sunday schools in England*, it may not be amiss briefly to state them.—In the first place he objected, not merely to the degree in which corporal punishment was inflicted by the masters of the schools, but to their power of inflicting it at at all, except by the authority, and in the presence of the visitor of the schools. He also suggested an increase of rewards, of such a nature as to be to them most acceptable, and *not distant in prospect;* recommending in a particular manner that most effectual, and most economical, of all rewards—PRAISE and COMMENDATION—wherever due ; and, in all cases, to be bestowed by the visitors and directors themselves.

In the distribution of the prizes to the children at the Sunday schools, the objects of reward, he thought, should not be *brilliancy of talent,* or even *proficiency in learning;* but that kind of merit which might offer to *every scholar* the ground of competition;—viz. *regularity of attendance, cleanliness of person, habitual diligence, and orderly behaviour;*—points, upon which the governors might decide with facility, and with unvaried impartiality.—In objecting to early hours, Dr. Briggs has not been biassed by a *fellow feeling for indolence;* as, notwithstanding his professional occupation, and his civil duties as mayor of Kendal, he has generally attended, as visitor of the Kendal schools, from SIX TO SEVEN O'CLOCK EVERY MORNING.

The governors adopted his suggestions; and they have been followed with as much success, as even an *ardent* and benevolent mind could have wished. It is a gratifying circumstance to the *Society for bettering the condition of the poor,* to be authorised to state, that the perusal of their Reports, published about that time, stimulated Dr. Briggs to pursue the success of his first attempt, by more extensive and effectual measures. He immediately applied his mind to form a general plan for the education and improvement of all the rising generation at Kendal, and produced the following detail, or outline, in the beginning of the year 1799.— First, that public schools should be established in Kendal, where all the children of the poor

might be employed during the day, in various
kinds of work, and from whence they might
return to their parents at night —Second, that
the scholars should be divided into a convenient
number of classes; and that each class should
be taken from work an hour every day, to be
taught to read and write, in a separate room,
by a master provided for that purpose.—Third,
that the scholars be entitled to the *whole* of
their earnings; subject only to a small fixed
deduction for school wages, less than what they
had been accustomed to pay at other schools.—
Fourth, that annual premiums should be offered
for the best specimens of the different kinds of
work.—Fifth, that to these schools a public
kitchen and eating room should be added;
where any of the scholars, who choose, may
dine comfortably at a cheap rate :—and, Sixth,
that a certain number of the elder girls should
be appointed to assist in the kitchen, by rotation.

In consequence of this proposal, a meeting
of the inhabitants of Kendal was called, on the
14th of February, 1799; Mr. Wilson, the then
Mayor of Kendal, being in the chair. The
plan was adopted, a Committee appointed, and
a subscription opened for carrying it into effect.

In May, 1799, the Committee gave notice of the opening of the schools, for the employment, and instruction, of children of three years old, and upwards; with the addition of a penny ordinary, for those who chose to partake of it.

The schools of industry at Kendal, contain one hundred and twelve children; whereof thirty of the larger girls are employed in spinning, sewing, knitting, and in the work of the house; and the thirty-six younger girls in knitting only. Eight boys are taught shoe making, and the remaining thirty-eight are engaged in what is called *card setting*;—the preparing of the machinery for carding wool; an occupation apparently difficult and intricate, but easily learnt, and peculiarly adapted to little children. For the industry schools there are two mistresses for knitting and spinning, at eight shillings a week each; and a master shoe maker, whose salary (arising out of an allowance of twopence a pair for finishing the shoes; and in fact decucted out of his scholars' earnings,) amounts to twelve shillings a week. For the reading and writing school there is a master, aged eighteen, at half a guinea a week; and an usher, *a boy of* fourteen, who was allowed eighteen pence a week, but, in consequence of superior offers, is now engaged at three shillings a week. These two, with the assistance of the upper and more intelligent boys, supply all the requisite instruction for these industry schools, where one hundred and twelve children are educated and fitted for useful life. The expense of the whole establishment, in salaries, fires, candles, rent, and every other incidental charge, (furniture, premiums, and school wages being deducted,) has amounted in two years to only 110*l.* 1*s.* 2*d.*; or 55*l.* 0*s.* 7*d.* a year.—For this annual expenditure, how much has been done, will be detailed in the remaining pages of this extract.; in which I shall direct my attention chiefly to those points, in which the schools at Kendal differ from other schools.

Of the boys, I have already stated that, eight are employed in making shoes. This is the most expensive part of the establishment, the extra expense of teaching these eight boys being something more than twenty guineas a year; so that if this were deducted, the cost of teaching the other scholars would not be so much as six shillings a year, or about five farthings a week each. But, perhaps however, this will be found to have answered as well as any part of the establishment; these boys being now, at the end of eighteen months, able to make shoes completely, except finishing with the knife, which is the last and most difficult part of the work. Some of them can even do this. The two best of these shoemakers *are both under twelve years of age;* and yet are capable, at that age, of earning, at Kendal, from three to four shillings a week each. One of these boys would, without any apprentice fee, be an acquisition, as an apprentice, to any master shoe-maker.

The girls schools are now, except as to their attendance on the reading school, entirely under the direction of a committee of ladies; who regularly visit and superintend them, and have produced an apparent difference in the cleanliness of their apartments, and in their personal appearance. The original plan for the instruction of them, in the different kinds of kitchen work, is in part executed. Breakfast is provided at the school daily, except on Saturdays and Sundays, for above forty scholars; each of whom pays fourpence halfpenny a week; a sum, which will barely defray the expense of provisions, without the fuel. The elder girls are employed, in rotation, to assist in preparing breakfast, and in washing the utensils. I was present at their breakfast to-day (10th of August, 1801), when abundance of very good milk porridge was served up, and partaken of by all the children, in a cleanly and decent manner. The object, which has been attained by providing the breakfasts, is the punctual attendance of the children in the morning; which had been frequently prevented by the real or pretended irregularity of their breakfasts at home.

Four of the girls have been, for two or three months, learning to wash. They bring their own family linen every Friday evening, being furnished with soap, fuel, and necessary accommodations, *gratis*. Two other girls have already been sufficiently instructed in it; and, in consequence have gone into service. Other girls are to be taught in their turns.

The Committee is preparing to erect an oven, and a baking plate; so that the girls may learn to make oaten cake, and wheaten bread. It is proposed that they shall then be encouraged to bring oatmeal and flour from home; so as to make bread and oat cake at the schools, for their respective families. This will not only be very useful to servants, but will also supply most essential qualifications for the wife of the cottager; so as to enable her to fill properly, and *economically*, the duties of her station in life.

The *mode of teaching the children their letters is deserving of attention. They are taught first to copy the capital letters in sand, from a printed card; beginning with the most simple forms, as I H T, &c. and proceeding to those that are more complex. They then learn to copy the smaller letters in the same way, and in alphabetical order. It is very curious to observe with what readiness and correctness the youngest of these children will form these letters in the sand; and how willingly they will make the knowledge of them a matter of amusement, and of self-gratification.

A set of maps having been presented and hung up in the school, Dr. Briggs adopted the idea of encouraging and stimulating the attention of the children, by giving them, every week, some easy lessons in practical geography. Those who have not visited these schools may probably doubt (as I did) of the propriety of making this a part of the education of *poor* children. Upon attending this morning, how-

* Dr. Briggs has the merit of being one of the first, who introduced Dr. Bell's mode of instruction into this country.

ever, I have had reason to appreciate highly the effects of this addition to their instruction; especially when I have considered, that these children might hereafter be placed in mercantile or naval situations, where this knowledge would be of essential use to them. I found indeed, that those, who answered best upon this examination, were the same who carried off the prizes of industry; and I had reason to believe, that, from the information and pleasure which they received in this instance, they transferred a spirit and energy to all their other occupations.

The queries were not put in an arranged series; but were varied in expression and order, and were always applied to the maps around them.—Nothing could exceed the air of intelligence, and the eagerness, and correctness, with which the children gave their answers, but the rapidity and precision of the questions put by DANIEL, THE USHER OF THE SCHOOL, (a boy of *fourteen years* of age, whom Dr. Briggs, then present, directed to make the examination) and the *severe impartiality* with which he passed on to the next child, if there was the least delay or mistake in the answer.

In the introduction of geography into his schools, Dr. Briggs had another very important object in view;—that of preparing the minds of the children for a system of RELIGIOUS IN-STRUCTION on a similar plan; so as to enable them to give a reason of the faith that is in them, whenever they may be assailed by SO-PHISTRY AND INFIDELITY. At our request, Dr. Briggs examined the children in sacred history, carrying his questions and instruction through the Old Testament; in a way, not only to open and improve their minds, but to afford instruction to my friend and myself, who afterwards agreed that we had never received a more useful lesson in sacred history. This second examination occupied the school until half past eight o'clock, when the children were summoned to breakfast.

A circumstance had occurred in the *Blue Coat* schools, which may shew how easy it would be, in *visited* and well regulated institutions, to make the elder children the teachers and instructors of the others. The school-master was compelled to ask leave of absence for a fortnight; and it was agreed, that his school must be shut up, of course. Mr. Dillworth Crewdson, one of the society of *friends* at

Kendal, determined to try the experiment of
putting the care of the school, during the master's absence, under *monitors,* selected from
among the boys; he and some others of the
governors *accidentally* looking in, and giving
occasional attention, according to their convenience. The event of the experiment has
been, that the school was as well conducted
during that month of the master's absence,
and the progress of instruction was as great,
as at any other time.

The benefit of the Kendal schools has been
much augmented by the willing and frequent
attendance of several of the most respectable
ladies and gentlemen of that place. This again
has received additional advantages from the
public examinations of the scholars, and from
the annual publication, not only of the names
of *the children* who have obtained premiums,
but of the circumstances relating to them.
More will still be done if a closer union takes
place between the *industry schools,* and the
blue coat schools; so as, not only to make the
one a preparatory seminary for the other, but
to propose the attainment of a place in the *blue
coat schools,* as an object of desire and ambition
to every child in the *schools of industry.*

Having extended to some length my account of the industry schools at Kendal, I shall confine my observations to one of the peculiar features of these charities ;—the employing of some of the scholars in aid of the general system of discipline. The whole plan of education in these schools, is carried on by a master aged eighteen years, employing some of the children to teach the younger part of the school, and having the aid of an assistant usher, a boy of fourteen years of age ; and it is conducted in such a manner as to make the success and progressive utility of the teachers, a spur to the industry of every other child in the school.

There are many and great advantages in employing scholars in every school, in aid of instruction and institution. The pupils are taught and improved, whilst they are teaching and improving others. Such assistants may be had without expense, and at the moment when they are wanted. They may be dismissed without any pension from the funds, and without any call for that pity which will, in some cases, induce governors of schools to vitiate the whole system, rather than discard or supersede an unworthy or incapable usher.

It has been observed that, whenever ushers

of *mature years* are *completely* fitted for teachers,
they are capable of earning a greater salary
than the school can afford ; so that all, who are
really fit for the situation, are looking out for
something better.   A similar circumstance may
attend those selected from the pupils themselves ; but what is an evil in one case, operates
as a benefit in the other.   The spirit of the
establishment, which has raised one boy above
the situation, has fitted and prepared * others
to succeed him.   Besides this, children, who
have been accustomed to exert themselves at an
early age in hope of advancement, will possess
more spirit, and more industry, than others
who have not had the same advantage.   They
will soon learn *to do every thing for themselves ;*
and will go into life with the habit of success,
with the due value of character and reputation,
and with the inestimable possession of active
and invigorating industry.

In order to calculate how far this theory may
be extended, let us suppose that an asylum be
formed for the education of the poor, on a scale

---

* The succession of new and *golden* fruit, to supply that
which is plucked off, will in this instance be as perfect, and as
uninterrupted, as in the fiction of the poet:

—— primo avulso, non deficit alter

Aureus; et simili frondescit virga metallo.

capable of receiving two hundred children ; or
" (to simplify the statement) two hundred boys.
—That their objects of attainment be reading,
writing. arithmetic, religious instruction, grammar, geography, geometry, navigation, astro-
nomy, and whatever else may fit a boy to be
useful in life.—That for this purpose, there
shall be the superintendance of one intelligent
director, who shall employ, for the care of the
school, a master, and two undermasters,* with
very moderate salaries ; not so much (with
respect to the under masters) to supply instruction, as to aid in the discipline of the schools,
to mark the regularity or attention of the scholars, and to note their punctuality or remiss-
ness in their daily tasks and attendances. That,
for the purpose of instructing these boys, fourteen of the eldest, or most intelligent, be
selected ;—that to one of them aged fourteen
years, with an assistant of twelve years old, there
be committed the care of the upper class, containing thirty four boys :—that to three other

---

* The under masters need not be, in point of literary attainment, on a footing even with the upper boys of the
schools.—For this office, some of the reduced serjeants of the
militia, or of the army, if orderly, well tempered, and properly
impressed with sentiments of religion, might be fitted as any
other class of men ; and their salary might be very limited.

boys of ages from eleven to fourteen, be entrusted the care and instruction of the three next classes, containing sixty-one boys;—that for the several other classes, where the instruction does not extend beyond mere reading (the letters being taught by writing in sand, as before mentioned) or beyond the elementary parts of writing and arithmetic, there be one master, aged twelve years and eight months, with seven assistants of ages from eight to twelve years.

Let us suppose that the business of these little teachers is not to punish, but to prevent faults; not to deter from misconduct, but to preclude it; and to use that influence, which children naturally possess over their immediate juniors, in forming and regulating the minds of their pupils; and that, when they shall have spent a year as teachers, they shall with pleasure move on to a superior class, into which they shall enter as mere scholars; increased, however, in diligence, in respect that they have been in the situation of instructing others. Let us further suppose that for boys so taught, and teaching. situations readily offer in life; and that few are not sought for before twelve years of age, as apprentices to some advantageous and useful trade.—But let the reader beware how he ventures hastily to reject all this, as *impracticable theory ;*—for it is a plain and literal account of the MALE ASYLUM AT MADRAS,—as it existed in 1796, under the superintending care of the Reverend **Dr. Bell.**

10th August, 1801.

No. IV.

DAY SCHOOLS AT WESTON.

In the year 1795, a free school,* for the education of the children of the industrious poor, in the village of Weston, near Bath, was established there by a lady; who has since succeeded, in forming and supporting four other similar schools, in the same village. The children are admitted at a *very early age*. They are kept very clean and neat: and, as soon as possible, are taught the Lord's Prayer, the *Gloria Patri*, and the Catechism. Their instruction proceeds until they can read, knit, mend, and make family apparel, and do all sorts of plain work. They attend the church regularly on Sundays; and those who are able, join in singing psalms in the church; forming themselves in a circle round their patroness, and vying with each other in exemplary decency of conduct. Her allowance for each child's schooling, is three shillings a quarter; a sum comparitively small, but yet supplying a very

* Reports, No. XCVII.

useful and acceptable charity, and contributing to the comfortable maintenance of five widow women; who thereby not only receive eight or ten pounds a year each, (the five schools containing near eighty children) but are also put in the way of receiving some additional benefit, from the credit of their situation in the schools.

I said that the children were admitted at *a very early age.*—The reader will be surprised when I add, that they attend the schools so early, as at two years old: each of the little ones being put under the tutelage and care of one of the elder children, and, as soon as they can speak, being taught the Lord's Prayer, and to be attentive and quiet during school hours. Their parents are, in consequence of their admission to the schools, enabled to go out to work, and to carry their labour to the best and most advantageous market.

She never keeps a girl in the schools after the age of twelve. By that time they are sufficiently advanced in reading, and in the use of the needle, to be of very great benefit at home; or, if not wanted there, to obtain advantageous situations in service. None of the children are allowed to take any pay for sewing work for their poor neighbours. That is all done *gratis :* and a useful charity is thereby engrafted on the original plan ; the children assisting in mending and making for all the industrious poor of the village. One of the primary objects of this lady is thus attained ;—the making of them, and of the other poor of the village, habitually kind and affectionate to each other. When, however, a girl can read and work *well*, and is able to make a shirt complete, she is then allowed to take employ from strangers, and to make a profit of her acquired skill in needle work.

In 1795, the time that this lady first began her system of education at Weston, there was only an evening service at the parish church on Sunday ; and that so ill attended, as to afford little encouragement to add a service in the morning. The regular and uniform attendance, however, of so great a number of children in the church, the introduction of psalmody by them, their leading the psalm-singing of the church, arranged in a choral body around their beloved protectress,—and the consequent attendance of many of the parents and friends of the children, did so increase the congregation, that a successful application was made to the worthy rector, to add a morning service. The parish church is now well and respectably attended twice every Sunday. A few years back, many of the parishioners never even entered the church doors: the sabbath was generelly considered merely as a day of leisure and riot. At present, small as is the parish, such is the regular attendance on divine service, that forty-four persons attended yesterday, being Easter-day, to receive the sacrament.

As soon as the children are old enough to understand what they read, this lady gives them prayer books, and instructs them how to use them at church. They follow the clergy-man in the responses; and in such good order, that a look from her is sufficient, without a word being said, during divine service. The whole of the Sunday she devotes to them: she hears and explains to them the catechism, and makes them repeat the collects: but she provides no other books of religious instruction than the Bible and the Prayer Book, and some selections from them; reserving the rest for oral communication. Of her method of communicating information on religious subjects, I can repeat an instance that occurred only last week.—A girl in her schools had just attended the funeral of her father, a pious and honest labourer at Weston. The lady took this opportunity of giving the children a lesson, on the resurrection, and a future state. " That child's " father," said she, " was on Tuesday last " placed in the grave : but he was a good and " religious man ; and we have a well grounded " hope, that, through the merits of Christ, he " is now in a state of glory and happiness. " He is indeed, separated from his child ; " but, if she is good and virtuous, and if she ' performs her duty to God, and to her neigh- " bours here, she will be received into the " same glorified and happy state, and dwell " with her father, and with the spirits of just " men made perfect, to all eternity."—

The infant age at which this lady receives the children, and the very early period at which she returns them to their families, or enables them to go into service, are features peculiar, in some degree, to the schools established at Weston, by Mrs. HOCKER ;*—the

* Since Mrs. HOCKER's death, I have the pleasure of stating that, by the exertions and attention of Mrs. GOOD-ENOUGH, and some other ladies, the WESTON SCHOOLS continue to flourish. There are at present in the five schools eighty-four children ; seventy-one girls, and thirteen boys.— The children are admitted from *three years* old, and are

lady, to whom that village is so greatly indebted for the instruction and education of
youth, for the comfort of mature and advanced
life, and for the religious improvement of all.
Those who have attended to the instruction
of children, have had frequent occasion to
observe that they are much more liable to
good and bad impressions, *at a very early age,*
than any *general system* of education in this
country seems to provide for. Many young
persons, as well in low as in high life, prove
decidedly vicious and hopeless, for want of an
early and active occupation, in something useful and satisfactory.

If I were to propose one pre-eminent object,
with which hardly any other could be placed
in competition, I should name EDUCATION :—
I do not mean that which only clothes and de-
corates the mind and body *with tinzel ornament,
and with imported frippery ;* and increases the
lustre of appearance in proportion to the decay
of principle,—as if, not merely in poetic fiction
enforcing a lesson of morality on this transi-
tory scene of life,—but that, in verity and

placed out in service at fourteen. B. 27*th Jan.* 1804.—Since
Mrs. GOODENOUGH's lamented death, these schools continue
under the protection of her sister, Mrs. SUTTON.—21*st Jan.*
1809.

reality of existence, *all the world were a stage,*
and we its inhabitants were all merely players ;—
and that the true and appropriate preparation of
life, were to fit us for no other duty or occupation, than to fill with grace and dignity a
place in its pageantry,—to act a part in some
vain and splendid exhibition,—and then be
seen no more.

To supply principle, to induce active industry, to promote the love of GOD and of our
neighbour, and to prepare us for our duty in
our allotted station of life—these are objects
of attainment to the rich, as well as to the poor ;
—objects, which attained (however lost and
hopeless may be the mature age of many in
every class of life), will for ever supply renovated youth, and unexhausted vigour to the
political body, and will protract to a distant
period,—otherwise beyond hope,—the duration and prosperity of this favoured empire.

It is worthy of observation, that the supply
of the Weston schools is not from the overflow-
ings of affluence ; but from the prudent and
self-denying economy of a small, and of a very
limited, income ; aided by the subscriptions of
the Rector of the parish, and of a few personal
friends of Mrs. Hocker. The great sacrifice

in undertakings of this nature, *where one indi-vidual ventures singly to take the charge of so large an establishment,* is time and attention; but, in the present instance, there must also have been a considerable self-denial in what is usually termed " gratification ;" in order to obtain, with means limited and inconsiderable, objects so desirable and satisfactory.

To those, however, who are inclined to try the experiment on the scale of *a single school,* supported either by one individual or by two or three friends, I can venture to affirm that they will find it a matter neither of expense or trouble; and that of all the amusements *they pay for,* this will be the *most economical and productive.* The union of any three ladies, in this work of pious charity, will, at the ex-pense of 4*l.* a year to each of them, afford education for twenty children,—will give com-fort, relief, and attachment, to almost as many poor families,—will assist the present, and im-prove the rising generation,—and will, at the same time, provide for some poor and honest widow * those means of occupation and liveli-hood, without which she might have been

* I will venture to recommend this mode of *patronage* to those who have, in instances, taken infinite pains to provide

compelled to be a burthen to herself and the parish.

There are some devout and well intentioned persons, who adopt a system, which rather seeks to mortify the soul by acts of penance, than to occupy it in works of utility ;—a system, that seems to attempt to extinguish the appetites and desires which our Creator has implanted in us, instead of labouring to correct their evil propensities, and to apply their potent influence to beneficial purposes.—Are we still to learn, that neither the appetites of man, or the pleasures of sense, were bestowed in vain?—that our passions and affections were designed, not to be the seducers to vice, but incitements to virtue? not to be the destroying tempest, but the *essential elements of life*, without which all would be a dead and destructive calm? " In order to " dispose the heart to devotion," (says a pious and eminent Bishop *) " the active life is to

for some distressed woman, by fixing her for life, as a *charge* on the funds of some charitable institution. They will find, upon a minute and correct calculation, that, without a regular canvass of the governors of a charity to induce them to act contrary to their trust, and with less expense, or discredit, they might have satisfactorily attained their object, by setting her up in some country school, to instruct the poor children around her.

* Bishop Wilson.

" be preferred to a life of contemplation. To
" BE DOING GOOD TO MANKIND, DISPOSES THE
" SOUL MOST POWERFULLY TO DEVOTION."
The poor are designed to excite our liberality,
—the miserable, our compassion,—the sick, our
assistance,—and the ignorant, our instruction."
—To this allow me to add, as a comment, the
consideration of what has been done at Weston.—The benefit there is not confined to the
succession of those who are preserved and
educated in the schools; the effects may be
traced as a salutary stream, pervading every
part of the parish.—The church is more frequented, the sabbath better observed, the cottager more thriving and comfortable, his family
better clothed, and every individual improved
by the example of those, who have received
benefit from these schools.

19th April, 1802.

No. V.

DAY SCHOOLS IN WEST STREET.

On the 3d of May, 1802, there were opened in West-street, in the parish of St. Giles, day schools * for two hundred children of the poor in that neighbourhood.   They have since been increased to the number of two hundred and forty children.   The schools are of the established church, and connected with the free chapel in West-street; and are either kept in the house adjoining the chapel, and belonging to it, or in the chapel itself, where the children attend at the times of divine service on Sundays, morning and evening, and Thursday evenings; and also on Thursday mornings, from nine o'clock to one, being the time fixed for their public examination.

For the education of each child, the parent pays, in advance, a shilling † a month.—It is curious that, in these payments, until the severe weather came on, there had scarcely occurred

* Reports, No. C.
† The payment is now reduced to ninepence a month.— 21 Jan. 1809.

an arrear of a shilling, from their first opening.
Some failures in payment have since occurred,
but not in many instances; and though the
payments amount to thirteen shillings a year
for each child, yet the rapidity with which those
vacancies have been filled up, and the applica-
tions that are daily made for admission of children, give some reason to believe, that, if the
school-house were adapted to receive five
hundred children, instead of two hundred and
forty, it would soon be filled.

As it will shew *one mode* in which *a general
and national system of education for the poor*
might be adopted at a very trivial expense, I will
state the outgoings of these three schools, and
the funds by which they are supported. The
only persons employed in them, are a master,
and two mistresses; dividing between them the
charge of two hundred and forty children, collected in three separate schools; each of which
occupies one of the three upper floors of the
house: floors which, it must be confessed, are
not sufficiently commodious for so large a number of scholars. The salary of the master is
50*l.* a year, and of the two mistresses 32*l.* and
30*l.* a year; which includes their board, and
every other incidental expense, except coals and

candles for the schools, and the cleaning of the house. For these three articles the master is allowed 16*l.* 10*s.* a year. The charge for house rent, &c. is 50*l.* a year. Of books, paper, &c. the annual expense is about 15*l.* To this will remain to be added the sum of 90*l.* for clothing ninety of the children, who are the nominees of annual subscribers of one guinea each, or of benefactors of ten guineas each.

Before I had stated the expenses of these schools, I should have observed, that there are also, on this establishment, Sunday schools for one hundred additional children, who are not paid for by their parents. The children of all the schools attend in the free chapel on Sundays,* and lead the psalmody of it with a degree of correctness and intelligence, that must surprise any one, who considers the short time which they have had to learn the tunes, and how unpromising scholars they must have been at first. Their progress is owing chiefly to the schoolmaster; who possesses not only a parti-

---

* This has increased the congregation at the free-chapel, not only on Sundays, but at the Thursday evening lectures; many of their parents *attending out of curiosity at first* to see their children, and to hear them sing. Of these parents, the greater part are now become regular frequenters of the chapel, and devout and attentive hearers.

cular talent for instruction in sacred music, but a singular pleasure in teaching it. The singing is also improved by a weekly practice after Thursday evening lecture, when Mr. and Mrs. Gurney, and their children, and about fifty of the congregation, join with much benefit and pleasure.

The total expenditure of the day schools and Sunday schools, being 283*l*. 10*s*. is provided as follows :—1st, by 84*l*. of annual subscriptions ; 2dly, by 156*l*. paid by the poor for their children's education, at thirteen shillings a year for each child ; and 3dly, by the collections of two morning and two evening charity sermons, producing together * about 50*l*. making together a total of 290*l*. and leaving a trifling balance to answer contingent expenses. When the cost of clothing the ninety children is deducted, the current expense of these schools for two hundred and forty children, and of the Sunday schools for one hundred childred (in so unfavourable a situation as the centre of St. Giles's), will not exceed by more

---

* The sermons are in May and November : the latter were on the 14th of the preceding month of November, when the collection, from an audience of one thousand persons, the greater part of them the poor of that neighbourhood, amounted to 28*l*. 11*s*. 6*d*.

than 37*l.* 10*s.* the payments which the parents do willingly make for their children's instruction.

In my observations upon these schools, I will exclude all general topics, and not trespass further on the time of the reader, than by a few brief remarks upon the peculiar features of *this recent experiment*, with respect to the education of the poor. It will not be easy to name a local situation where the remedy was so much wanted, and where circumstances were so adverse to the success of the experiment: and yet through the conduct and attention of the Rev. Mr. Gurney, and the intelligence and assiduity of the master, Mr. Neeves, and of his wife, and the other school mistress, these schools have, within nine months from the first proposal of them, been established with a success which promises increase both in number and effect. It may be proper to inform the visitor of the school, that if he is desirous of viewing a splendid establishment of pupils, a striking arrangement of building and appendages, and a surplusage of well appointed instructors and attendants, with handsome salaries and commodious apartments, he will find nothing of the kind in West-street. The size

of the house, the extent of its funds, and above
all, *the object of the experiment* (which is to produce a practical mode, in which the advantages
of education may be universally extended to
poor children at a very moderate expense)
have made those funds, which in some parts of
England, would not have been adequate to the
sustaining of a single master, with one insulated
pupil, the means of clothing ninety children,
and of extending the blessing of education to
two hundred and forty, and of supporting a
Sunday school * for the additional number of
one hundred more children.

The visitor should be prepared to enter
school rooms, apparently too small for the
number of scholars; but yet without any sensible inconvenience attending them, while they
are regularly cleaned and ventilated —He must
expect to see a number of children, many (except on Sundays) in mended, and some in torn
apparel; but if he will attend the progress of
the school, though he will not perceive any
forced and immediate change in children who

* The Sunday Schools are occasionally diminished in
numbers by a circumstance, by which in effect they are promoted and encouraged; the vacancies in the day schools being
preferably supplied from the most deserving children of the
Sunday schools.

have been so long neglected, yet he will view
with pleasure their advancement in cleanliness,
decency, and order ; and his observation of the
progress which he sees making, will probably
induce him to give credit for something having
been already done.

The effect of the Thursday's examination,
which continues from nine to one o'clock, in
giving energy and activity to the children's
minds, is very striking. In the last instance in
which I attended it, there were two hundred
and twenty children, ranged in eleven rows in
the pews, in front of the clerk's seat, which was
occupied by Mr. Neeves, the master ; the two
mistresses being attending in the side aisles.
One row, consisting of rather more than twenty
children, stood up at a time. The employment of that morning was the church catechism;
divided into short queries, and attended with
explanatory observations, and questions, on the
master's part. When each child had been
examined in its turn, another row stood up, the
attention of the children having been previously
relieved, by their all singing a verse or two of
some psalm or hymn.

On another day, they were employed in
reading the 6th chapter of St. John's Gospel,

accompanied with similar questions and expla-
nations,* addressed to them in such a manner
as to fix their attention, and to improve their
understanding. A lady, who has several schools
under her protection, was so much struck
with the manner and *effect* of this examination, as to request Mr. Neeves to endeavour
to prepare a written specimen of it, in order
that the experiment might be tried in her own
schools.

It is to the very general establishment of
parish schools in Scotland, and to the power
thereby given to parents to obtain the essential
part of education at a moderate expense, that
the Scotch are indebted for a very valuable part
of their national character. " North Britain,"
(says a Scotch writer,) " struggles with many
" natural disadvantages ;—the climate is cold,
" the sky seldom serene, the weather variable,
" the mountains bleak, barren, rocky, often
" covered with snows, and the general appear-
" ance of the country very forbidding to stran-
" gers ; yet *by an early attention to the education*
" *of youth, to form good men and good citizens,*
" she has uniformly maintained a high character

* This account was written in 1803. The plan and
management of the school has been considerably varied since
that time.—*1st March*, 1809.

" among the nations; has been always deemed
" an excellent nurse of the human species;
" and has furnished not soldiers only, but
" divines, generals, statesmen, and philoso-
" phers, to almost every nation in Europe."

Feb. 4, 1803.

No. VI.

DAY SCHOOLS IN THE BOROUGH.

In 1798, Mr. Joseph Lancaster opened schools * in the Borough road, Southwark, for the instruction of one hundred children of mechanics, in reading, writing, and arithmetic. They are now attended by five hundred scholars, and preparations are making for two hundred more. Only thirty are children of persons in a more independent situation. The peculiar modes of instructing the children, of exciting emulation by rewards, and of preserving order by division of attention, are such as merit a more detailed account than the plan of our work admits. This detail, however, the reader will find in a publication of Mr. Lancaster's, intitled, " Improvements in Education, as it re- " spects the industrious Classes of the Com- " munity."

In order to produce a stimulus to exertion, the master provided about two hundred leather tickets, gilt and lettered, according to relative

* Reports, No. CXVIII.

degrees of merit. The value of these tickets vary, from No. 1, which must be obtained six times to entitle the bearer to a halfpenny prize ; to No. 6, which gained forty times gives a shilling prize. The prizes consist of bats, balls, kites, and the like. Besides this, there are in the schools honorary orders of merit, worn by the pupils until forfeited by misbehaviour ; the forfeiture being in lieu of corporal or other punishment.

The system of tuition is almost entirely conducted by the boys ; the writing books are ruled with exactness, and all the writers supplied with good pens by the same means. In the first instance, the school is divided into classes ; to each of these a lad is appointed as monitor. He is responsible for the morals, improvement, good order, and cleanliness of the whole class, and it is his duty to make a daily, weekly, and monthly report of progress, specifying the number of lessons, of boys present, absentees, &c. &c.

As the boys who are acting as teachers, are expected to leave the school as soon as their education is completed, they are instructed to train other lads as assistants who may supply their places, and in the mean time may leave them more leisure to improve in other branches of learning.

The office of monitor is at once honourable and productive of emolument. There are besides, other lucrative offices of trust. The monitor delivers out the gilt and lettered tickets, a second the tickets of merit, another has the general charge as to cleanliness, &c. and a fourth has the care of the 500 slates. Thus every duty has its respective officer, and the fidelity and assiduity displayed in their discharge is surprising. This system of tuition is mutually for the advantage of the lads who teach, and of those who are taught. If a lad in one class becomes qualified for removal to a higher, he receives an appropriate reward, and his monitor also a similar one. The same regulation takes place in arithmetic on going into a new rule. The advantage derived from entering the daily reports of progress made by each class is considerable; it obliges the monitors to go straight forward, without wandering from one lesson to another; and it affords, by inspection, a true account of the lessons, &c. performed by every boy, and also a view of the general progress of the whole school

The method of spelling is among the most

useful of their improvements. It commands attention, gratifies the active disposition of youth, and is an excellent introduction to writing. It supersedes, in a great measure, the use of books, while it greatly increases the improvement of the scholars. It is as follows:—Twenty boys are supplied with slates and pencils, and a word pronounced for them to write. They are obliged to listen with attention to catch the sound of every letter, and have to connect this with the idea of each letter, and the pronunciation of the word, as they write it on their slates. Now these twenty boys at a common school would each have had a book, and one at a time would have been reading or spelling to their teacher, while the other nineteen were looking at their books, or perhaps entirely idle. On the contrary, when they have slates, one boy may read to the teacher, while the other nineteen are spelling words on the slate. The class by these means will spell, write, and read at the same instant of time. In addition to this, the trouble which teaches twenty will suffice to teach 60 or 100, by employing some of the senior boys to inspect the slates of the others, they not omitting to spell the words themselves, and on a signal given by them to

the principal teacher, that the work is finished
by all the boys they overlook, he is informed
when to dictate another to the class.—By an
experiment recently made, it was found, that
the word THANK was written by 296 boys, and
the examination made by the master and monitors, in the space of one minute; and the
word ALCORAN in two minutes and an half.
Near twenty of the boys who wrote these words
could scarcely form a letter ten days before.

The following method has been adopted
with success in teaching arithmetic. The cy-
pherers are in distinct classes: the monitors
of the class having a written book of sums which
the scholars of his class are to do, and another
written book containing a key to those sums.
In the first place, when the boys of his class
are seated, he takes the book of sums, suppose
the first sum in Addition to be as follows:

lbs.

5432
4567
5432
4567
5432
2222
———
27652

He repeats audibly the figures 5432, and

each boy in the class writes them; they are then inspected, and if done correct, he dictates next the figures 4567, which are written and inspected in like manner, and thus he proceeds till every boy in the class has the sum finished on his slate. He then takes the key, and reads as follows: first column, 2 and 2 are 4, and 7 are 11, and 2 are 13, and 7 are 20, and 2 are 22. Set down 2 under the 2, and carry 2 to the next. The above sum was, a short time since, written by 116 boys and inspected by their monitors in twenty minutes: many of them had finished in fourteen minutes. The whole of a sum is written in this manner, and read by each boy in the class; it is afterwards inspected by the monitor, and frequently by the master; and it is a method peculiarly well adapted to facilitate the progress of the scholars in the elementary parts of arithmetic.

Multiplication is easily obtained in the same way; and the scholars by writing acquire a thorough knowledge of numeration, expressed both in words and figures, without paying any attention to it, as a separate rule. The boys vie with each other in writing their sums neatly on the slate, and their improvement in writing becomes greatly increased. Another great and

important advantage derived from this plan, is
the certainty to the teacher, that every boy in
the class is employed, and that none sit idle
while others are waiting the master's partial
instructions ; and three times the usual number
of sums are done and repeated by every boy,
while no inconsiderable degree of competition
is excited.

The new method of spelling already described, only applies to those who can write ;
but in all large day-schools there are many
children who have not acquired this art, and
who are sent to school solely to learn to read.
To obviate this difficulty the following plan,
nearly similar to that which has been successfully practised by Dr. Bell, in the Male Asylum
at Madras, and mentioned in the account of the
schools at Kendal,* has been adopted. The
scholars have a desk before them, with ledges
on every side, and it is filled with sand to a
level with these ledges. Every boy is furnished
with a sharp-pointed wire to write, or rather to
print with. A word is then dictated by the
monitor, for instance BEER, and it is immediately sketched in the sand by every boy with
the point of his skewer, and when inspected

* See the Reports of the Society, No. XC.

by the monitor, another word is dictated. It possesses part of the advantages before described, to be attached to spelling on the slate. This class of children lose more than two-thirds of their time, when taught in the usual method.

The importance of moral and religious instruction is too evident to admit of a question. To promote it in a manner the most economical, to augment the happiness of the scholars, and to induce them to make the most beneficial use of their time, are objects highly deserving of consideration. When a general system of education is become so very desirable, and is so much desired, it is therefore no small merit for Mr. Lancaster to have introduced a method, which to the economy of time and attention, adds a very great pecuniary saving. The expense of his school, including books, rewards, slates, &c. does not amount to 7*s*. 6*d*. a year for each pupil. In the usual mode of teaching sixty boys, they would require sixty slates, sixty spelling-books, and thirty bibles. In Mr. Lancaster's school, the same number of boys have only two bibles, three spelling books, and sixty slates; being a saving of £6. 7*s*. 9*d*. or above four-fifths of that part of the expense.

4th June, 1804.

No. VI.

DAY SCHOOL AT CAMPSAL.

THE school for poor children at Campsall,* in the county of York, was established by three young ladies, the daughters of Mr. Frank; who undertook, as soon as their own education was completed, to instruct at their father's house, a few poor girls in reading, plain work, and knitting; and they likewise gave them some necessary articles of clothing. They have been since induced by the solicitations both of the poor children in their neighbourhood, and of their parents, gradually to increase the number of their scholars; and it now amounts to between sixty and seventy, all of whom they teach themselves.

On Sundays, the children attend the school in the morning and afternoon, and go regularly to church; where they have been much noticed, on account of the neatness of their appearance, and the propriety of their behaviour. On week days, the school hours are from nine in

* Reports, No. CXXV.

the morning till noon, and from one till four in the afternoon. All the children are taught reading, knitting, and plain work; and such as appear most capable of improvement, are also instructed in writing and in accounts. Great pains are taken to make them acquainted with the leading principles of religion and morality, and with the peculiar duties of those useful, though humble stations in life, which it will probably be their lot to fill.

They seem in general to make as much proficiency, in the various branches of their education, as could reasonably be expected; and appear gratefully attached to their benevolent teachers, whose instructions they receive with much satisfaction, as well as docility. In these respects, the distribution of little rewards for improvement has produced so powerful an effect on their minds, as to have rendered any other method of exciting diligence, and ensuring regular attendance, almost unnecessary.

The age at which children are admitted, and the time they may continue in the school, are not fixed by any general regulations. The attendance there is perfectly voluntary: it is not expected during harvest, or at any other time when their parents can find more profitable employment for them, or particularly need their services at home. They are permitted to bring work to school, when their parents or friends can supply them with it. When they are not thus provided with employment, they are furnished with work by the ladies, and are allowed the usual price for it. This was for some years paid them in money, as soon as each article was finished; but it was determined a few months ago, to keep their earnings till the end of the year, in a box provided for that purpose, with a separate division for each girl; and then after deducting the payment of a female friendly society which has been established by the Miss Franks, to give the value of the remainder in some of the most useful articles of clothing; as shifts, petticoats, &c. These they are taught to cut out, and to make at school; for which purpose, and for knitting their own stockings, three weeks are allowed. None of the parents have expressed the slightest disapprobation of this alteration, in the manner of disposing of their children's earnings. The children themselves appear highly delighted with it. Many of them remember exactly how much money they have in the box, and are very solicitous to add

to their stock. Some of them persuade their
parents to pay for them the contribution to the
friendly society, in order that there may not be
on that account any diminution of their little
hoards. It is hoped that these little funds,
besides answering their immediate purposes,
will form them to habits of industry and frugality, that will continue through life; and
that many of the possessors will, when engaged
in service or other business, very frequently
replenish the private fund of the above-men-
tioned friendly society, by placing in it small
sums of money at interest.

These young ladies furnish their scholars
with work at home, as well as during school
hours; being chiefly the making of gloves,
knitting of stockings, and also shoes and socks
for infants; to which of late has been added
platting of split straw. The articles which the
children make, are in a few instances disposed
of to shopkeepers, but more generally to private persons, who are disposed to encourage
the charity. During the summer months many
are sold at Askeron; where a collection of
them is kept by a poor woman, the mother
of eight children, four of whom attend Miss
Franks' school.

The clear profit derived from the sale of the articles made by the children, after deducting from the price received, the cost of the materials, and the payments to them, together with some small presents of work from a few ladies, contribute to form a fund, for providing various rewards for diligence and good behaviour in the school ; and for furnishing a donation in clothes and useful books, together with a small sum of pocket money, proportioned as exactly as possible, to the length of time they have attended the school, and to their general deserts, on their becoming servants or apprentices.—

The foregoing account is a striking example of the effects of industry, directed to the most useful ends, and unremittingly applied. That three young ladies should by their own exertions, in a few years form, and bring to perfection a school of above sixty girls, *conducted without the assistance of mistresses*, and regulated only by their personal superintendance, (besides establishing a friendly society, combined with their plan, and calculated to extend its benefits), so much surpasses the ordinary effects of benevolence, as to excite emotions of surprise when the fact is first mentioned. How much ought it to operate, in repelling the ordinary excuse of inactivity or irresolution,—the want of means or opportunity to do good? It does not appear, that any collateral circumstances of influence or situation, have given any peculiar advantages to these ladies, in the execution of their plan; but it appears to have arisen at first from a very small beginning; the establishment having been gradually enlarged to its present extent. This will afford encouragement to benevolent undertakings, that the amount of benefit ultimately to be derived from them, may very far exceed whatever could at their first outset be foreseen.

This account will also point out a mode, in which, at a very limited expense, a large establishment may, with constant attention, be conducted. It will prove how much may be effected by the exertions of those whose moderate circumstances may place expensive contributions out of their reach:—that diligence, animated by benevolence, will create the funds. which, when furnished by indiscriminating bounty, are too often misapplied:—and that the labour of the poor, even among children, may be so directed, as to supply the means of their own instruction and improvement.

To ladies, whom the duties of their families

activity or situations may preclude from undertaking an extensive plan of instruction, it affords
a valuable example of the advantage of gratuitous
tuition, though confined to a small number of
children. There are few who might not effect
something in this way, without too great a sacrifice to their time, or encroachment on their
necessary employments; and it is impossible to
calculate the effect of such disinterested benevolence, upon the feelings and habits of the
poor, as well as on their improvement in useful
acquirements. The respect and attention, with
which poor children, receive the instruction of
those whose rank is elevated above their own,
co-operate with the superior qualifications of
these teachers in point of education or knowledge; while the gratitude, which must be in-
spired by such a beneficent attention to their
welfare, cannot but excite them to prove themselves worthy of the patronage they have received, by a diligent practice of the virtues in-
culcated upon their minds.

In the detail of the plan, though it bears
evident marks of the good sense and ability with
which the whole has been arranged, yet there
are many circumstances which have arisen from
local convenience, and which might not be

applicable in different situations. The general principle of a system of rewards and distinctions of merit, constantly operating, is however in almost every possible case of the greatest importance ; and has in the present been found sufficient to supersede all compulsory means of enforcing attendance, and almost to preclude the necessity of having recourse to punishment. This system may be variously modified, so as to suit different establishments. but it can scarcely be thought possible that the vigour of the human mind should be efficaciously called into action, especially in children, but by the immediate prospect of advantage and reputation, held out to them in forms suited to their capacities, and captivating to their imaginations.

1st March, 1805.

No. VIII.

DAY SCHOOL AT BERHAMPORE.

WHILST the 53d regiment was stationed at Canterbury, in the beginning of the year 1805, a few children of the regiment, of both sexes, were assembled in the house of one of the officers, and received a little instruction from his family; but the removal of the regiment broke up the school, and it was not assembled again till the regiment was stationed at Dinapore, in the East Indies, in March, 1806.

A school * was then formed, under the patronage of the Colonel of the regiment, upon

* We are indebted for this account to Mrs. Sherwood, the daughter of the late Rev. Dr. Butt. Her letter contains an account of a religious society in the 22d regiment, which we have much pleasure in adding in her own words.—" I have within a few days been much delighted with a little society, in the 22d regiment; which is come to this place to remain here, in lieu of the 53d regiment. These poor men, about twenty in number, had formed themselves into a small club or religious society, when placed in Fort William, in Calcutta, some years ago. They were allowed a bomb-proof room to retire to, and an old schoolmaster, of the name of Edmonds, read to them, prayed with them, and sung Psalms. The rules of their society are won-

a regular plan. One of the serjeants, who
could read and write well, was appointed to be
master of the school, and the children were assembled in one of the virandas of the pay-
master's quarters, in order that the family
might have an opportunity of frequently

derfully pure, simple, and strict; such as might have suited a
company of saints in the apostolic ages; no genteel vice whatever being allowed. Whoever breaks through these rules, is
banished the society; and is not re-admissible, but with the
approbation of every individual of the society. When the
regiment was removed from Fort William to Cawnpore, (as I
understand, on foot, not in boats) the society had few opportunities of meeting; and the members felt that they were
gradually losing the spirit of religion. One evening, stopping
at Alahabad, they after a long march, met in a grove of man-
goes at midnight; and continued the whole night in prayer
with one accord, and singing of psalms; making the Indian
groves, and the shores of the Ganges, resound with the praises
of a Redeemer. They said that the refreshment and comfort,
which they found this night, was wonderful; and in the morning they continued their march with joy.—There have lately
been some disturbances in the 22d regiment, of an unpleasant
nature, which, by the prudence of the Commander in Chief
will, I hope, be amicably settled. These poor Christians, on
this occasion, acted in a manner worthy of their calling.
Since their regiment is come to Berhampore, Mr. Parson,
the chaplain of the station, has provided them with some
apartments in his grounds; to which they retire morning and
evening to read and pray. Mr. Parson frequently visits them.
It is delightful to hear their songs of praise, in this region of
idolatry and blasphemy: for the dreadful wickedness of this
unhappy country cannot be described."—*August*, 1807.

directing the master, and inspecting the children.

The children of the regiment who vere fit for instruction did not amount to above eighteen, including two or three sons and daughters of officers, and three or four little drummers. Each of these children pay a sum of the value of sixpence to the master, and the hours of attendance are from nine till one in the afternoon. The heat of the climate will not permit them to attend the school again in the afternoon.

The children are taught by the master to spell, write, and cypher; he also instructs them in classes according to Mrs. Trimmer's plan, making use of her Teacher's Assistant. The little girls have been for many months instructed in needlework, apart from the boys, in the same house, by one of the ladies of the regiment; and the boys have also received instruction in reading from the same person. The larger boys are also taught to write regimental orders, in the same manner as this business is carried on in the Orderly Room. The master reads aloud a part of an old book of orders, whilst the scholar commits what he reads to paper. Two or three of the boys are able to perform this exercise with tolerable accuracy.

When these children first came to the school, few of them could tell their letters, and one only could read. Most of the boys now read the New Testament with ease, and are by no means slow in comprehending what they read. Their manners also, from being perfectly wild and licentious, are become decent and submissive. This improvement is particularly remarkable in the boys. But it has been observed with regret, that the improvement of the girls, notwithstanding the pains which have been taken, has been far less remarkable : the private habits of a barrack being much more injurious to the minds of females, than to those of the other sex.

Upon the whole, the patrons of this school have met with more success than could have been expected : although the children are still, it is feared, very far from possessing that truly Christian spirit, which should be prized above all learning. But it is the duty of those who have the care of children (in whatever situation they may be placed) diligently to plant and water, humbly trusting that God will in his good time give the increase.

No. IX.

INDUSTRY SCHOOL AT OAKHAM.

RULES FOR THE SPINNING SCHOOL* AT OAKHAM, RUTLAND.

1st. ALL inhabitants of the parish to be admitted.

2d. No persons to receive relief from the parish upon account of their families, who refuse to send their children to the school: unless they can prove, to the satisfaction of the overseers, that they can employ them to more advantage elsewhere.

3d. They are to be instructed gratis in spinning jersey, and linen, and in knitting: those who choose it, in reading; and those who can bring work with them, in sewing.

4th. The hours of work to be from eight to one, and from two to seven; from one to two, dinner and rest. No work after dinner on Saturdays.

5th. A dinner to be provided for those who

* Reports, No. IV.

choose to dine at the school on the working days ; for which they are to pay each sixpence per week.

6th. In case of illness, the dinner may be sent for to their homes.

7th. The portions, if the dinner is sent out, to be as follows :

One pint and half of peas porridge.

Ditto   ditto of rice milk.

Ditto   ditto of rice broth.

One pound and half of potatoe pudding.

Those, who dine at the school, to have as much as they choose to eat, and a quarter of a pound of bread each ; except on the pudding and rice milk days, when no bread is allowed.

8th. The whole of the earnings to belong to the children.

A spinning school had been established at Oakham, in 1787 : but, till this arrangement took place, the children used to go home to their dinner ; which was attended with great inconvenience in wet and bad weather, and with loss of time ; as, frequently, when the weather was very bad, they did not return after dinner ; and sometimes did not go at all.

In order to establish the present system, the dinners for the first fortnight, were given gratis, and the parents invited to taste them; after that they were informed that the children of those who approved of the plan, *might* dine there, upon paying *sixpence a week;* and those, whose parents preferred their dining at home, *might* continue to do so. The whole of the parents approved much of their dining at the school ; and the whole number, which amounts to between sixty and seventy, dine there, and pay their money. They do more work in the week by these means, and get a much better dinner than they could at home. Several children come there, whose parents do not receive relief.

By purchasing the different articles wholesale, by the use of barley bread (which is customary at that place), and by means of a Rumford copper, the expence for the dinners and fuel has never exceeded the sixpence per head.

The peas porridge, and pudding, are taken from Count Rumford's book, with some alterations, which made them rather more expensive, but certainly better.

I conceive that the success, which has hitherto attended this plan, is owing to its having been left to the *option* of the parents, whether their children should dine there or not.

16*th March*, 1797.

No. X.

INDUSTRY SCHOOL AT LEWISHAM.

In April, 1796, a meeting of the inhabitants of Lewisham was called, for the purpose of setting up a school of industry,* for the children of that parish. The subscribers came to a resolution to prepare accommodations for the reception of sixty children, and the house was opened on the 30th of May, 1796.

The children are admitted on the recommendation of subscribers, and by order of the Committee. In summer the school is open from six o'clock in the morning to six at night, and in winter during the hours of daylight; but the children have usually finished their task by two o'clock; they then go away, unless, which is the case with some of them, they *prefer* to work additional hours *on their own account.* They receive two meals a day, a breakfast and a dinner; one hour being allowed at dinner, and half an hour at breakfast. They are employed in spinning, winding, and knitting;

* Reports, No. XXIX.

and one boy in weaving. The present weaver is an active boy, not ten years of age : his predecessor had been employed but a very little time, before he had an offer of a permanent engagement at a cotton mill. In rotation they all receive lessons in reading. The children's weekly maintenance is estimated at 1*s.* 6*d.* per head ; and where they earn more in any week (as some do 6*d.* a week, and some 1*s.*) they are paid, and carry home the overplus. One little boy (who came from the workhouse with but a bad character, but who now possesses a very good one), earns not less than an extra shilling a week ; he has during the last month, put into the master's hands, in trust for him the sum of 5*s.* In the case of the parish children, who are entirely maintained at the parish expence, there is, as yet, no certain allowance ; but they are rewarded according to their industry and good behaviour. It is however in contemplation to make them a certain allowance ; probably a sixth of their earnings.

Spinning wheels are lent, and materials are furnished at home, for any of the adult inhabitants of the parish, who wish employment; and they are paid for their work upon delivery. A suit of clothes, made of the cloth and camblet of their own manufacture, is yearly given to each of the children, who attend the school, as a reward for their good behaviour, and to enable them to appear decently and regularly at church on Sundays.

In the infancy of a manufacture, there is necessarily a loss from the waste of raw materials. In the present instance it must be admitted, that very little profit accrued from the labour of the children, during the first six months: but, for the next half year, the profit was gradually increasing: and it advanced so much, that at the end of the year, on the 30th of May, 1797, the net profit of the manufactory had amounted to 55*l.*—That profit may be fairly stated at 100*l.* a year in future. The school of industry now supplies the parish workhouse with most of their articles of clothing: besides which, a stock of knitted stockings, and of camblets and worsted, is kept in the warehouse, to be sold by wholesale and retail. The demand for them has been gradually increasing; and the inhabitants have found their advantage in the purchase of them.

The weekly expense of the family, upon an average, is 3*d.* a head per day; including the twenty parish children,* and the master and mistress, and their two children, who have their three meals a day, and lodge in the house For each of the parish children, the establishment is allowed the sum of 3*s.* a week ; which is near 50*l.* a year less than the expense of merely feeding them in the workhouse during the preceding year.

The following is a pretty correct estimate of the expenses and receipts of the establishment.

PAYMENTS.	*l.*	*s.*
Maintenance of the family, clothing, &c. - - -	250	0
Wages of master and mistress, 10*s.* per week. *He is extremely well acquainted with every process in the woollen manufacture* - -	26	0
School mistress; who teaches the children to read - -	3	0
Rent of the house, and the wooden building behind. *It was a blacksmith's shop, but is now the school and work room* - - -	13	10
	292	10

* This number occasionally varies ; there have been twenty three in the school at a time: but the number will probably be much less.

	l.	*s.*
Brought over,	292	10
Insurance - - -	1	0

Mr. Hall, the manager, who does not live in the house, but attends occasionally. *He purchases the provisions, and materials for the work, and provides a sale for the articles of manufacture*   -   -   -   **30 0**

Incidents, gratuity to the secretary, &c.   -   -   -   **26 10**

	350	0

RECEIPTS.

Parish rents appropriated to the Institution,   -   -   -   **60 0**

Allowance for twenty parish children, at 3s. a week each,   -   -   **156 0**

Profits of manufactory per annum; supposed   -   -   -   **100 0**

	316	0

Deficiency in the infancy of the establishment to be made good by subscription   -   -   **34 0**

	350	0

There are 48 persons, including the master and mistress, and their two children, who

breakfast and dine regularly in the house. The
table of diet, and quantities allowed for them,
which are quite as much as they wish, are as
follows :

Monday. Breakfast. Rice milk ; made of 4lb.
of rice, 1lb. of flour, 1lb. of sugar,
and 4 quarts of milk.

———— Dinner. 20lb. of beef, and a peck of
potatoes, with 17lb. of bread.

Tuesday. Breakfast. Broth, and 13lb. of bread.

———— Dinner. Boiled rice ; consisting of
15lb. of rice, 1½lb. of sugar, and
3 quarts of milk.

Wednesday. Same as Monday.

Thursday. Same as Tuesday.

Friday. Breakfast. Gruel, made of 2 quarts
of oatmeal, with the allowance of
1lb. of butter, 11lb. of bread, and
¼lb. of salt.

———— Dinner. Beef stew ; consisting of
22lb. of shins of beef, and a peck
of potatoes, with 17lb. of bread.

Saturday. Same as Tuesday and Thursday.

The workhouse children, and the master's
family, (in all 24), have for their Sunday
breakfast, gruel, made of one quart of oatmeal, with the allowance of half a pound of

butter, 8lb. 10 oz. of bread, and 4 oz. of salt;
for dinner, 12lb. of beef, half a peck of potatoes, 5lb. 5 oz. of bread, 8 oz. of salt, and 3
quarts of beer; for supper on Sunday, 6lb.
8 oz. of bread, ½ lb. of cheese, and 2 quarts of
beer, and the same supper on the other days of
the week, with a little additional allowance of
bread, of which they seem to require more on
week days than on Sundays. The price of the
beef is 3s. a stone, or 4½d. per pound; of the
two shins of beef (weight per average, including bone, 22lb.) 2s. 6d.: of potatoes 20d. a
bushel; of their bread, which is good seconds,
7½d. the quartern loaf, or rather more than 1½d.
a pound.

By the preceding bill of fare, it will appear,
that the cheap article of rice now forms a very
considerable proportion of the children's diet.
The use of it has been gradually increased,
partly in consequence of their having acquired
a greater fondness for it than for other food, and
partly from the observation of its nutritive and
wholesome qualities. Its average increase, on
boiling in mere water, has been found to be
fourfold: with the addition of milk, it is much
more.—The good health, which the children
have uniformly enjoyed has been remarkable;

several of them, who were weak and sickly at their admission, have since become healthy and vigorous ; to which their new habits of cleanliness and regularity, and the exercise of spinning by hand wheels in an airy apartment, as well as their diet, which is nutritious and plentiful, may probably have conduced. The improvement in their morals and behaviour, has been equally satisfactory to the wishes of the promoters of the Institution. It is found that, in proportion as the children become skilful and useful, their parents and friends, learning their value, become desirous of withdrawing them, because they can employ them to more advantage.* This has already been the case of

* Upon a visit to the Lewisham School of Industry, I had procured a list of the children employed, and the amount and profit of the work done by each, with a view of inserting it in these notes: but upon repeating my inquiry a few weeks after, I learn that some of their best hands had gone out, apprentices to trade, or into service, in consequence of improved habits and character; and that there is not one now in the school of the age of twelve years. Even the little weaver, *in the tenth year of his age*, has accepted *an advantageous offer in his own line*, and quitted the school. Circumstances like these, must always check the progress, and diminish the profits, of manufactories in industry schools; but they shew the value and real benefit of those establishments, as nurseries of useful members of society, instructing and enabling the poor to obtain the most useful and acceptable relief,— that which comes from their own industry and good habits. B. 18*th April*, 1798.

many, and generally has happened in the course of six months after they have been received into the school ; as the habits of order and industry, which the children acquire there, render them so desirable as apprentices, that, though there has been a difficulty heretofore in finding situations in private families for any parish children, because *they come out of a workhouse,* yet they are now sought for, and the parish is relieved from the expense of their maintenance at a much earlier age, than if they had been kept in the workhouse.

One other very great advantage resulting from this establishment, and from its necessary connection with the poor of the parish, is, that the gentlemen, who have interested themselves in its success, have thereby been induced to take a very active part in the management of the poor ; and one of them, Robert Saunders Esq. is now serving the office of overseer for his second year. It will be obvious that a great benefit to the poor, and a considerable saving to the parish, must be the consequences of such an institution. The poor are more happy, and better taken care of than they were before ; and the saving, from the new system, will hardly be less than 500*l.* a year.

By the preceding account it will appear, how much may, at a very small expense, be effected by a judicious and spirited adoption of one of the measures, directed by the statute 43d Elizabeth. It is needless to observe upon the effects which this establishment has necessarily produced on the morals, the cleanliness, and the health of the children ; who, being now habituated to industry, instructed in reading, and accustomed to a regular attendance on divine worship, are bred up in the knowledge and practice of obedience and reverence to their Creator, and of that utility, which he has enjoined as a duty to their fellow-creatures.

Besides the advantage of separating the parish children from the contagion of those dissolute and profligate characters, which are to be found in all workhouses, the maintaining them at a less expense, and the educating of them in the habits of industry and virtue (circumstances which apply to the parish children removed from the workhouse to the school of industry), it should be observed, that a very great relief is also given to the other poor of the parish, by easing the parents of the burthen of maintaining so many of their children, and by giving the mothers profitable employment at home ; a relief, that by improving the circumstances of the cottager, has a just and honourable tendency to reduce the poor's rates.——Establishments, like that at Lewisham, have also the merit of correcting the little pilfering habits of the infant poor, the source of so many vices and crimes in society ; and of preserving them from idleness and bad example, and training them in virtuous and industrious habits, so as to make them blessings to their parents, and useful and valuable members of society.

22d Feb. 1798.

No. XI.

INDUSTRY SCHOOL FOR GIRLS AT BAMBURGH.

Sixty poor girls,* elected from the township and neighbourhood of Bamburgh, in the county of Northumberland, are taught to spin jersey and flax, to knit, to sew, and to mark ; and are also instructed in religion, psalmody, reading, writing, and the elementary parts of arithmetic. None are admitted under the age of five years. Twelve of the youngest are only taught reading and knitting; the remainder are divided into two sets (of twenty-four each, when the school is complete) which are alternately employed for a week at a time in two rooms, superintended each by a different mistress.

The lower room is about forty feet long, twenty feet broad, and above twenty feet high. This is wholly appropriated to spinning ; the jersey spinners occupying the floor with twelve wheels and a large reel ; and the flax spinners employing the like number of foot wheels, on

* Reports, No. XXXVII.

an open gallery about seven feet high, erected for that purpose along one side of the room, so that the mistress has a full view of the whole number at once. These are again subdivided, so as to work three days in the week on the gallery, and the other three on the floor.

The upper room, for sewing and knitting, is about eighteen feet square; it is high and well lighted on three sides. Here the youngest girls do no other work than knitting: the twenty-four eldest sew in the morning, and knit in the afternoon.

Besides the two mistresses attending these two rooms, a master is employed in a smaller room near the sewing school, in their instruction as above mentioned. For this purpose, the whole number is divided into six classes, of ten scholars each; these classes, being taken in rotation from the works, and remaining with him each one hour a day. He likewise reads an appropriate form of prayers to the whole school every morning, and keeps the account of their absences, and of the after mentioned tickets. On Sundays the scholars of both schools assemble in the boys' school, where a preparatory form of prayer is used, and a psalm sung; after which they go down in procession with their masters and mistresses to the parish church, where seats are provided for them.

There are apartments for the two mistresses and master, among the buildings occupied by the female school of industry. The salaries of these three teachers, and the expenses of fuel for all the apartments, are defrayed by the trust.

The whole profit of the work is divided among the scholars; a small part weekly, but the bulk of it annually at Christmas, in the following manner. The mistresses and master have tickets to distribute among them *daily*, according to their diligence and good behaviour; and to be withdrawn or diminished on account of any fault, according to certain rules printed for their use; and the annual distribution of profit is made in exact proportion to the number of tickets that each scholar has received and preserved during the year.

These girls attended only as day scholars until the latter end of last October; when twelve of them, between the ages of seven and nine, were admitted as inmates, to be provided with food, clothing, and lodging, at the expence of the charity; towards which, however, the profits of their work are re-

ceived. They chiefly consist of children living
at too great a distance to attend the school;
and, in the election of them, a preference
was given to orphans and other destitute
children. They are meant to remain until
they are fourteen or fifteen years old. A cow
is kept for them, which, in the last year or two
of their time, it is intended they shall milk;
and that, as they advance in strength, they
shall occasionally, and in turns, be employed
in washing and mending their own clothes, in
dressing their victuals, and in cleaning the
rooms; by which means they will be prepared
for good services, which it will be the endeavour of the trust to procure for them, with
suitable encouragement for their employers and
themselves. There is every reason to hope
that the produce of their work will so much
diminish the expense of their maintenance, as
to enable the trustees to extend this benefit to
a greater proportion of the whole number, without much additional charge to the charity.
Every one of the twelve, now admitted on this
footing, had knit herself one, and some two
pair of stockings, and was completely taught to
spin jersey within the first quarter, though not
instructed in either of these works before.

Nothing now remains but to state the methods taken to provide employment. The greatest difficulty was in respect to sewing. In order to bring this kind of work within their reach, handbills were distributed in the neighbouring towns and villages, giving notice that it would be carefully performed at one half of the usual rates; and, by the good management of the mistress, it was so well executed, that work soon came in, and still continues, from all quarters, as much as can be executed, if not more. And the reduction in price, in respect to young servants and unmarried labourers, is found to be as much a charity to the purchaser, as to the children employed.

The flax is bought on the best terms; and, when spun, it is woven and bleached in the parish. By the care of the mistress and the weaver, in sorting the thread according to its quality, the cloth has been all very good and serviceable; and, after allowing the children the usual spinning prices, has abundantly re-paid all the charge of materials and workman-ship.

Wool is purchased of the farmers after shearing time; and a large room, with all pro-per conveniences, is appropriated to the use of a manufacturer, who is employed in sorting, dying, and combing it. The jersey, when spun, is doubled by some of the children ; and then brought back to the combing room, where there is also a twisting mill for finishing it as worsted. Part of this is sold, part employs the knitters, and some is sent to two stocking weavers at Berwick ; and it does not appear that there will be any difficulty or loss in the sale, either of the stockings, or of the worsted.

The produce of the tickets at Bamburgh school, is distributed in money. In general, it is preferable to bestow it in articles of cloth-ing : as, in many parts of England, the fathers would carry the money to the alehouse, or the mothers buy finery for themselves. In Nor-thumberland, such are the good habits and economy of the poor, that there is no danger of such a misapplication ; and, upon the first introduction of work into the school, it was found expedient, by the allurement of a pay-ment in money, to engage the parents' consent to it, instead of their children being employed, as at first, in reading, writing, and arithmetic, the whole day.

The manner in which work has been pro-vided for this school at Bamburgh Castle, is extremely deserving of attention, on account of its being practicable and beneficial in every part of England. It not only removes the great difficulty in the support of schools of industry, that of obtaining regular employment for the children, but affords a cheap supply of clothing for the neighbourhood.

The providing of dinners for the day scholars of schools of industry, at a very cheap rate, is very useful in other counties; but it is not so much so in Northumberland, as the poor in the North have the advantage of possessing more management and economy with regard to their food, than those in the other parts of England.

There is also a school at * Bamburgh for sixty boys. The account of that, and of some other

* This school at Bamburgh Castle, is one of a great variety of charities, established under the will of Nathaniel, late Lord Crewe, and Bishop of Durham, who died in 1722; having devised considerable estates, in the counties of Durham and Northumberland, to five trustees; charged, in the first place, with the annual payment of some noble and well known benefactions to the university of Oxford, and to Lincoln college, of which his Lordship had been Rector; and of several sums for the augmentation of livings, and the institution of schools, almshouses, and for other beneficent purposes, in the several counties and parishes, with which he had been connected; the residue being applicable to such charitable use and uses, as the trustees should from time to time appoint and direct.—This surplus was accordingly applied for various purposes of charity, as opportunity offered; but, during more

parts of the establishment at Bamburgh, may
form subjects of future communications to the
society.

than thirty years after the testator's death, it does not appear
that any *permanent* and regular system was adopted.   It was
about that period that the ancient castle of Bamburgh, once
the residence of the kings of Northumberland, and situated
on one of the trust estates, began to be repaired ; first for the
purpose of holding the manor courts, and as a habitation for
the minister ; and afterwards as the fixed seat of several charitable establishments of great extent and utility, chiefly planned
by the late Dr. John Sharp, Archdeacon of Northumberland,
and Prebendary of Durham, who was elected a trustee, in the
room of his father, Dr. Thomas Sharp, in the year 1758;
from which time, till his decease, which happened in 1792, he
was employed in arranging, with the concurrence of the other
trustees, these plans, which he carried into execution with
great zeal and promptitude, superintending every part of this
administration with indefatigable perseverance : for which
purpose he resided in Bamburgh Castle during several months
in every year.   And, in order that his successors might find
every encouragement to continue these good works, he not
only expended a good part of his own property, in his lifetime,
on the improvements and accommodations of the place, but
at his death, bequeathed to the trustees all his furniture there,
and a large and valuable library, besides a freehold estate, and
a considerable sum of money, to be vested in the funds, for
the perpetual repair of the great tower or keep, which he
occupied, and intended for their use.

No. XII.

INDUSTRY SCHOOL AT FINCHAM.

In October, 1802, a school* was opened at Fincham, in the county of Norfolk, for the education of the children of that and the adjoining parishes. They are instructed twice a day in reading, and eight of them in writing. The rest of their school time, being seven hours of the day, is employed in the platting of split straw; for which, in addition to the advantage of education, they receive pay, according to the amount of their respective earnings.

There are at present in the school sixty-four children. Four have left it to go into service, and seventeen have acquired a competent knowledge in the straw platt, and have returned home to their parents. The school is under the care and direction of three sisters; who have divided it into three classes, making the undermentioned weekly payments on the aver-

---

* Reports, No. CXII.

age to each of the children, for the time they are employed in the platt.

Nineteen children, from seven to nine years
    old, average each per week -   1 6
Twenty-seven, from nine to twelve years
    each   -   -   -   3 0
Eighteen, from twelve to fourteen years
    each   -   -   -   4 0

All the children are in good health, clean and orderly. The produce of their work is sufficient to supply (after the first month) the average payments before mentioned, without any deduction, except 3d. a week for each child who learns to write. These allowances for children who really work but seven hours a day, and whose ages are from seven to fourteen,* amount on an average to as much as 2s. 10d. a week for each child, exclusive of the benefit of instruction and education.

The school is very frequently visited by the Rev. Mr. Forby, the vicar of Fincham. He very kindly allows himself to be referred to, as a kind of judge or arbitrator, upon any matter

---

* Children who live near the school, go home to dinner, from twelve to one o'clock, and lodge at home : of the others, some bring their dinners, and return home at night; others lodge at Fincham, and are at home only from Saturday to Monday.

arising in the school; and, in case any of the children have been neglectful and inattentive, he makes use of his influence to amend and improve them, and to prevent a repetition of the cause of complaint.

In the fourth volume of the Reports of the Society, the reader will find some observations on the manufacture of split straw, with instruc-tions for those, who may be disposed to intro-duce it into parishes, for the employment of poor children. To such persons this account of the Fincham school is addressed; as affording an example of the manner, in which provision might be made, in almost any part of England, for the education of all the poor children, and particularly the females,* of a neighbourhood, with very little trouble or expense.

The benefit which the children receive from their admission into this school is very consider-able; inasmuch as, without that excess of labour or confinement which is exclusive of amuse-

---

* Dr. Briggs has introduced the split straw manufacture, as a part of the girl's employment, in the Kendal schools. Several of the girls now earn two shillings and sixpence a week by it, though they give up part of the day to needle-work. He observes that, if it be sufficiently lucrative to keep the girls at school, that will be very satisfactory; and it promises to do that, even at as low a price as one shilling and sixpence the score.

ment and injurious to health, it provides for
their education, and prepares them for their
course through life, by early habits of ORDER,
CLEANLINESS, AND APPLICATION,—the three
most essential articles of acquirement.—To
parents it is of no small importance ; in that
it fits their children to get their own bread,
while young ; and by the profits of their work,
supplies, at present, almost all the expense of
their food and clothing, at an age when they
are too young to go into service.—What are
its advantages to the public, will be obvious to
those, who are aware, how much we all suffer
by the pilfering and profligate habits of our
little parochial pensioners ; and how large a portion of our parish funds (sufficient, perhaps, to
give education and employment to all the poor
in England), is annually expended in breeding
up and nourishing in *idleness,* those who, in
mature and advanced age, are destined to form
the *helpless* and *noxious* part of the community.

The beneficial influence on this school, from
the frequent visits of the clergyman, is of too
much moment to be passed by without notice.
In all ages and ranks of life, it is very essential,
that we should respect the justice and impartiality of the government to which we are sub-

jected. There is a degree of restraint and coercion, which cannot be dispensed with in schools ; and in reconciling the minds of this little flock to something so opposite to the unrestrained idleness in which they have hitherto been indulged, the visits of a person who has had no previous bias, and the impartial interference of such a character as the resident clergyman of the parish, must have the best and most salutary effects.

In supplying the *idle* with employment, and in seducing them to take the benefit of it, it frequently occurs that the *industrious* are checked in their exertions, and prejudiced in their means of life. When, for example, the needlework of a district is engrossed by a parish workhouse or by a charitable school, and the work is to be disposed of to the neighbourhood at an underprice, the solitary sempstress, who has been striving to maintain herself by being useful and industrious in her own cottage, is thereby deprived of her livelihood, and is reduced to the degraded situation of a pauper. This is an evil, which is more or less incidental to every plan for employing the poor, except in those cases, where *new occupation* is devised and introduced. Such, in an eminent degree, is the manufacture of split straw; which, while it gives food and employment to the idle and unoccupied, does not interfere with any means of subsistence, which the industrious and well disposed do at present enjoy.

The objection * to split straw, as a durable and permanent article of manufacture, has been already noticed in the Reports. There seems no reason to apprehend the discontinuance of the *material*, as an object for fashion to mould and shape into all its variety of fickle and capricious forms.—Let us, however, for a moment imagine that, after the prevalence of a few years, it *may* go into disuse. If in the interval (and I will calculate upon even so short a term as five years) we can make it the instrument of giving instruction to the rising generation, and of education of a succession children, *for five*

* See Report, No. CVI.—The manufacture of split straw is making a considerable progress at present, and that of the Leghorn platt is already begun by Mr. Corston, who has five acres of very promising Leghorn wheat, near Swaffham, in Norfolk, for the express purpose of this manufacture. It cannot be too frequently noticed, that we should endeavour to make the straw manufacture, the means of education for the young, and of occupation to infirm persons who are not fit for other work.

years only, in habits of *order*, *cleanliness*, *ap-plication*, and *usefulness*, it will confer on this country one of the most important advantages it has ever received.

No. XIII.

INDUSTRY SCHOOL AT BIRMINGHAM.

THE expediency of separating the children *
of the poor, from those depraved and incorrigible persons who too frequently form the
population of a parish workhouse, had induced
the overseers and guardians of the poor at
Birmingham, to place such as were from four
to ten years of age, with nurses in the neighbouring villages. This however was attended
with some inconveniences. The attention of
the overseers and guardians was then directed
to another object. A large building, about a
mile from the town, was vacant. This suggested
the formation of a separate establishment; and
an offer having been made by some of the guardians to conduct it, the new establishment commenced in July 1797.

A matron was appointed; who, with a
school master and mistress and one female servant, formed the household. The elder girls
have assisted in cleaning the rooms, making

* Reports No. CXXIII.

the beds, &c. a kind of employment, which, while it ministers to general economy, improves them all in a most useful branch of domestic education. The girls have been taught to read; and have been employed in knitting, needlework, &c. for the asylum and the work-house, and for respectable families; and such credit have they had for the manner in which their work has been done, that more has been sent them than they have been able to execute.

In summer, the boys have been occasionally sent to labour in the farms and gardens, in the vicinity of the Asylum, and to weed and pick stones. The produce of this, with the work of the girls, has formed a little fund, which has enabled the Committee to build a shop;* where forty boys are employed by a pin-maker to head the pins, and stick them in papers in rows. By the further increase of this source of labour, they have also built another room, where forty girls are employed by a respect-able draper, in platting straw for ladies' hats and bonnets. The overseers and guardians are

* The profit of these children's work, from January, 1800, to July, 1804, has been 576*l.* 4*s.* 4*d.*;—the expenditure in building, repairs, &c. 348*l.* 10*s.* 7*d.*;—leaving a balance in the Treasurer's hands, in July, 1804, of 235*l.* 10*s.* 9*d.*

now going to enlarge the pin shop, so as to include forty boys more in that manufactory,

Besides the produce of their labour, these children do now acquire early habits of industry and subordination, to which they were before entire strangers; for, previously to this attempt to civilize these forlorn and unhappy creatures (most of whom had never known the reciprocal endearments and powerful operation of parental and filial affection) their rude and savage manners, and disregard of authority, had produced habits so untractable and turbulent, as for some time to baffle every effort of the Committee to correct them.

The first expedient, which contributed at all to this object, was the placing of them in classes, and conducting them in order round the governor in the play ground, several times a day; when he had an opportunity of marking their individual conduct, of correcting the disorderly, and of applauding the tractable. This has been followed by placing them in order at meals; and by every other measure that occurred, for impressing upon them ideas and habits of order and regularity. The good effects of these measures were daily more and more apparent; and these children are now become as orderly and as decent, as such a number of children, under one roof, can ever be expected to become.

They have also a Sunday service regularly and decently performed by a respectable young man, a clerk in the workhouse, who concludes with reading a sermon. On this service the whole family attends with much order and propriety.

The children have meat three times a week. They have also soup, puddings, rice, milk, bread, cheese, and beer; and these the best of their kind. The medical gentlemen, who are employed for the workhouse, attend weekly in succession, and two physicians of the town have benevolently given their services when called upon.

The Committee, five in number, meet once a week at the Asylum, for the regulation of the accounts, and for the general superintendance of the whole. Each takes a department in providing the various supplies; making himself responsible for the quality, quantity, and terms, on which the articles are purchased. Thus the children are better kept, and with more economy, than by any preceding plan.

The great object of this institution is even-

tually to place these children in society, with
the advantage of better habits and propensities,
than would have been derived without some
such preparative education. And such has
been the effect of the means applied, that they
who had once been the pest and dread of
housekeepers and manufacturers, are now
sought for with avidity, as orderly and useful
servants, and have every opportunity afforded
them of enjoying a comfortable and permanent
subsistence.

These are certainly great advantages ; especially as they have been obtained, not only
without cost, but have been attended with the
saving of a sum so considerable as 3000*l.* in the
space of seven years, computed from July,
1797. The detail of the account is very correctly stated in the report of this charity, published in October last. I have therefore inserted it in a note.*

The great and essential benefit of the foregoing plan is the SEPARATION of the parish
children from those hopeless and depraved
characters, which constitute too great a part of

* PARISH OF BIRMINGHAM.—The following is a copy
of the ANNUAL STATEMENT made by the ASYLUM COM-
MITTEE, of the expenses, and calculated savings, with the

the population of every workhouse. The reader should be aware that these children continue to be maintained by the parish. But he
will find that the expense of that maintenance
in the seven preceding years, has been less by

average number of children each year in that establishment,
from its commencement in July 1797, to July 1804, inclusive.

FIRST REPORT. *July* 1798.

Savings to
the Parish.

£. *s.* *d.*   £. *s.* *d.*

The average number of children 248, if *put out* to nurse
would cost the parish 2*s.*
each per week   -   1289 12 0

Their maintenance, including
rent, fire, wages, &c. at the
the Asylum, at 1*s.* 4½*d.* each
per week, cost   -   884 2 0
                                          405 10 0

SECOND REPORT. *July* 1799.

The average number of children 290, if at nurse would
cost 2*s.* each per week,   1508 0 0

Their maintenance, at 1*s.* 4¼*d.*
each per week, cost   -   1021 8 5
                                          486 11 7

THIRD REPORT. *July* 1800.

The average number of children 269, if at nurse would
cost 2*s.* each per week,   1748 10 0

Their maintenance, at 1*s.* 10*d.*
each per week, cost   -   1283 1 4
                                          465 8 3

3000*l*. than it would have been in the parish workhouse.

As the account now stands, the parish has made an annual saving of above 400*l*. a year;

Fourth Report. *July* 1801.

	£.	s.	d.	Savings of the Parish. £.	s.	d.
The average number of children 281, if at nurse would cost 3*s*. each per week,	2191	16	0			
Their maintenance, at 2*s*. 1½*d*. each per week, cost	1555	14	6			
				636	1	6

Fifth Report. *July* 1802.

	£.	s.	d.	£.	s.	d.
The average number of children 250, if at nurse would cost 2*s*. 9*d*. each per week	1787	10	0			
Their maintenance, at 2*s*. 4¼*d*. each per week, cost	1532	1	4			
				255	8	8

Sixth Report. *July* 1803.

	£.	s.	d.	£.	s.	d.
The average number of children 200, if at nurse would cost 2*s*. 9*d*. each per week,	1430	0	0			
Their maintenance, at 2*s*. 2½*d*. each per week, cost	1153	10	8			
				276	9	4

Seventh Report. *July* 1804.

	£.	s.	d.	£.	s.	d.
The average number of children 235, if at nurse would cost 2*s*. 9*d*. each per week,	1680	5	0			
Their maintenance, at 1*s*. 11½*d*. each per week, cost	1196	10	10			
				483	14	2
				£.3009	3	11

—has sent out their poor children with the means and ability of maintaining themselves; —has diminished the profligacy, and improved the habits and industry, of their neighbourhood; and in that class of young persons, who in many other parishes are daily proceeding

Beside the above savings in the maintenance of the children, they have made considerable earnings in labour suited to their ages; the boys, in the heading of pins and sticking them in rows; the girls in weaving straw for ladies' hats, knitting stockings for the workhouse and asylum, mending linen, &c. The smaller children are employed in making oakum from old ropes; the elder females contribute to the general comfort by their labour in the house, which reduces the establishment to a governess, schoolmaster, and mistress, and one female servant. Their habits of industry produce a cheerful subordination, and render them more acceptable when called into any service in active life. Their health is also much benefited by the order in which they live; for many weeks in succession, not one is to be seen on the sick list, and seldom more than one or two at a time; few in such a number have died, and none are oppressed with hard labour, so as to produce deformity, which was not uncommon while under the care of hireling nurses in the neighbouring villages. —It might be observed, that the view in making this report public, is not only to shew the town, that considerable, and not unsuccessful efforts are made to mitigate the burthens of parochial taxes; but at the same time to prevent, in some measure, their recurrence, by uniting profitable labour with useful habits, in this branch of the rising generation—" the children of the poor." It was likewise considered, that it might afford some useful hints to neighbouring parishes, to prove that the moderate labour of children is not only productive of present profit, but of permanent and extensive benefit to the parish, and to society.

from idle habits to atrocious crimes,—has had
the gratification of observing a gradual and uninterrupted progress in habits of industry and
prudence, and in the practice of morality and
religion.

5th Jan. 1805.

No. XIV.

INDUSTRY SCHOOL FOR GIRLS AT CHELTENHAM.

THE Cheltenham School * of Industry, for girls, under the patronage of HER MAJESTY, was instituted in 1806. The scholars are divided into three classes. The FIRST consists of twelve girls, who are called *Fund Girls;* being the children of the most deserving parishioners, from ten years old to twelve, selected on its first institution, from among those who had the best characters in the Sunday schools. Two of them are nominated by the Patroness. They are admitted on the fund every three years, and are clothed.

THE SECOND CLASS consists of girls, that are paid for by their parents, at the rate of twopence a week. This class consists of twelve girls, from eight to nine years old. In respect

---

* This account has been communicated by Mrs. Williams, of Prestbury, near Cheltenham, the founder of this school, and is now first published by the Society.

of their clothing, they have the same advantages as the *Fund Girls*. They may remain in this class three years; at the end of which, they have the privivilege of being removed into the first class for three years more ; and in case of the death, or the removal of any girl from the first class, from any circumstance which may have occasioned it before the appointed time, her place shall be filled from the second class, by one chosen for *merit*, and referring to the number of rewards which she may have had in the preceding year.

THE THIRD CLASS consists of girls nominated by subscribers. Every subscriber of a guinea is intitled to send a girl to the school for one year.—The girls must be able to read before they are admitted into the school. They are taught knitting,—spinning flax, hemp, and jersey ;—platting whole straw for baskets,—cutting out and making clothing for the poor ; —washing, ironing, baking, milking, and household work ; so as to make them not only useful in farm houses, but capable of being under housemaids and kitchen maids in large families, or upper maids in small ones.

Any *Fund Girl*, who has remained two years in her first place, on a certificate of good beha-

viour, is intitled to a Bible, marked " *Reward*
" *Bible, Cheltenham School of Industry*," and to
two shifts, and two pair of stockings.

Girls who have been at the school of industry,
and any young woman who may want employment, are supplied with work, and paid for it,
by the school ; but this is under strict limita-
tions, to prevent their depending on work, when
they are capable of going to service. The annual subscriptions defray the current expences
of the school : the donations are applied to the
benefit of the outworkers, and to the supply of
materials for work and clothing. Those who
receive parish relief, or neglect attendance on
church, are precluded from the purchase of
cheap clothing.

For the public rules of the school, and the
private regulations, we must refer the reader
to the printed account, which is sold for the
benefit of the charity. They are directed with
considerable attention and arrangement, to give
the girls habits of devotion and cleanliness, and
to enforce regularity of attendance, care, and
exertion, by frequent examination, rewards, and
well grounded hope of future protection. A
little library is kept, which the upper girls are
allowed to borrow for Sunday evening, but to

be returned the next day.   Four girls of the
upper class act in rotation every six weeks, as
the houshold servants of the house ; and three
other girls, with the appellations of *Work Girl,
Book Girl,* and *Bonnet Girls,* take care of the
articles to which their titles apply.

The object of this charity is to promote religion and industry among the female poor,
by early impressing their minds with a just
sense of the importance of both, to their present
as well as their future happiness ; and to place
them more effectually above the necessity of
being tempted to swerve from rectitude, by
enabling them in various ways to earn an
honest livelihood.—Besides baking, milking,
washing, ironing, and every kind of houshold
work, they are taught to spin, to knit, to sew,
to plat whole straw for baskets, to cut out and
make clothing, which is afterwards sold to the
poor at reduced prices.   The school also gives,
under certain restrictions, a stated price for
work, to any girls or young women who apply
for it, and might otherwise, perhaps, for want
of employment, fall victims to idleness and vice.

24th Jan. 1809.

No. XV.

SUNDAY SCHOOL AT KIRKSTALL.

ABOUT three miles * and a half from Leeds, near the remains of Kirkstall Abbey, and on the banks of the river Aire, is a small hamlet, consisting of ten or twelve families, all of them having a number of children. The fathers of these children are most of them employed at the forge, a neighbouring manufactory for cast iron ; the mothers in general cannot read. There is no place of divine worship nearer than two miles ; and Sunday was generally spent by the inhabitants, in sauntering through the woods, or about the ruins of the abbey. With a view to remedy this neglect of the Sabbath, a small school has been instituted there on Sundays. One of the cottagers, who has himself seven children, and who has a roomy house, has been induced to act as master, for which he is very well qualified. A few benches and books constituted the whole of the

* Reports, No. CXI.

original expense of the school. The master
thinks himself amply rewarded by receiving
a guinea at Christmas, together with a few
clothes for himself and family. Such parents
in the neighbourhood, as are induced to take
advantage of the institution, and are from circumstances able to pay, are expected at Christmas to contribute a trifle towards firing. Every
person willing to conform to the rules of the
school, by regular attendance and decent behaviour, is invited to send his children. Neglect of attendance, and want of obedience, are
faults for which, if persisted in, the children
are discharged the school. Thirty children,
from five to fourteen years of age (being an
equal number of boys and girls) were there
yesterday, Sunday, April 17th, decent in their
appearance and behaviour, and many of them
already able to read very well. Children,
under the age of five years, are also permitted
to come; and attend with great willingness,
thereby acquiring habits of quiet attention, before they are capable of learning. Several of
the elder inhabitants avail themselves of this
opportunity to hear the Bible. The whole
place has now a very different appearance on

a Sunday; and the hedges and birds-nests escape on that day, at least, from the depredations consequent to total idleness. A few books are occasionally given, as rewards for regular attendance, and good behaviour. Some children come from so considerable a distance as two and three miles, and are remarkable for regular attendance. There are, at some seasons, above forty scholars thus instructed, with very little expense and no trouble. The school commenced in June, 1801. Convinced that time bestowed on these establishments is of much more consequence than the money they may cost, the institutors of this little school, have made a point of visiting them as regularly, as distance well permits in winter; and, when on the spot in the summer months, at least once every Sunday, hearing the children read, and themselves bestowing the trifling rewards.

The above is deserving of notice and imitation, in every part of England. There is no mode, in which so much benefit may be conferred with so little expense and attention; whether we look to the education of the young, to the comfort, improvement, and religious habits of the old and middle aged, or to what is sadly neglected in many parts of England,— the due observance of the Sabbath.

18th April, 1803.

No. XVI.

SUNDAY SCHOOLS AT DROMORE.

In the Sunday Schools * which the Bishop of Dromore has established in his neighbourhood, children of all persuasions are admitted, and in considerable numbers. On a Sunday, when I visited the Bishop last autumn, there were above one hundred children assembled on the lawn in the front of his Lordship's palace, half a mile from the town of Dromore; and they were all carefully examined and rewarded according to their merits. I have since learnt that they frequently assemble there in far greater numbers; and I have received the following particulars concerning the establishment of these schools.

There are five Sunday Schools in the parish of Dromore; two of them entirely supported by the Bishop. He contributes to the three others, giving occasionally to them all, books and other premiums. Twenty years have

* Reports, No. CXLII.

passed since he first established them. Having for a few months tried the effect of a certain number of children of the religious persuasions, he had a meeting of some of his own clergy at an examination of the schools, uniting with them the Roman Catholic Priest, and two Dissenting Ministers of the different congregations, called here old and new lights.* With them was settled a plan of instruction, for instilling the fundamental principles of Christianity, chiefly taken from our Church Catechism; and for teaching them their duty to God and their neighbour; impressing them with a particular abhorrence of lying and theft.— The effect has answered his most sanguine expectations; the surrounding peasantry being now remarkable for their truth and honesty.

Every Sunday morning the children attend their teachers in the school-houses; and after Divine Service, three and sometimes four of the schools (the fifth being too remote) assemble with their masters, as is above mentioned, before the Bishop's Palace. Every one

---

* The Old Lights strictly adhere to the Calvinistic Doctrine. Both agree in the same Presbyterian Church government.

that can answer the question proposed is rewarded with a halfpenny; afterwards they withdrew with the greatest regularity, arranged two and two together; the first step towards improvement being to accustom children to a respectful, decent, and orderly demeanour. They are also required to come neat and cleanly, and the Bishop has given amongst them for a Christmas gift, a gross, or twelve dozen of combs. The children of all the poor families around him, whether their parents be Roman Catholics, Dissenters, or of the established Church, are all equally desirous of receiving this instruction, and of enjoying these benefits, of which they all partake without distinction. In order to remove every prejudice, the Bishop is not so exactly scrupulous in the choice of masters, as to confine them entirely to members of the established Church; but he is careful to see, that they strictly follow the plan of instruction, which had been prescribed; and for that purpose they are constantly examined by his own Agent, and inspectors appointed by himself; and he has never found that any undue advantage has been taken of his confidence in the teachers.

The members of the established Church form here a very respectable and large congregation, which has so increased, that it has been found necessary to make the addition of another aisle to Dromore church. This church was rebuilt after the Restoration, by that excellent prelate, Dr. Jeremiah Taylor, then Bishop of Down, Connor, and Dromore, and author of many valuable works, particularly his Rule of Holy Living and Dying. In this church he was buried.—There are also two large congregations of Dissenters, distinguished as above, and one of Roman Catholics, not so numerous. To the erection of their chapel, and to the rebuilding of one of the meeting-houses, the Bishop contributed. Indeed he pays the kindest attention to the Dissenting Ministers, and to the Roman Catholic Priest, whom he frequently invites to his table; and whenever the Titular Bishop visits this part of the diocese, he is always invited, with his clergy to Dromore House. By this, and by a variety of other instances of conciliating and liberal conduct, he has produced the greatest harmony among his neighbours. They are no less distinguished for their loyalty; so that a well disciplined corps of yeomanry having been formed he never once, in the late rebellion, quitted his residence there, during the whole of that alarming period.

No. XVII.

ENDOWED SCHOOLS AT CHESTER.

THE income of the Blue Coat School * at Chester, had for several years been applied to the maintenance and education of thirty boys, who were admitted at nine years of age, and kept in the house for four years. This provision had proved to be extremely inadequate to its object; the greater number of the poor of that city being left entirely destitute of instruction. In 1783, the trustees adopted a beneficial extension of the charity: and in the course of that, and of the ensuing year, they opened a day school, in a wing of the hospital, for the instruction of one hundred and twenty boys in reading, writing, and accounts. This they call the *Green School*, from the circumstance of each of the boys wearing a green bonnet. Two masters were engaged, one at 35*l.* the other at 30*l.* a year; and they have proved quite equal to the care of the one hundred and twenty boys. The whole expense of teaching

* Reports, No. LXI.

these boys, including their bonnets, &c. is not more than eighty guineas, or 14*s.* a year, each.

In order to provide for this expense, the Trustees diminished the number of boys in the Blue Coat School, from thirty to twenty-five; and at the same time extended the benefit of that school to a great increase of objects, by reducing the time of continuance to two years, and by selecting the best behaved and most deserving boys of the *Green School* for all the vacancies in the *Blue Coat School;* so that twelve or fourteen of the best boys of the former school are annually placed upon the foundation: the consequence of which is, that there is hardly any poor boy in that city, but may obtain a place in the Blue Coat School, if he perseveres in a course of industry and good behaviour.

This is of the greatest importance; as it extends the benefit, not only of instruction, but of (what is much more efficacious) emulation and example, to almost every lad in Chester. The boys are now admitted at nine years of age into the Green School, upon the nomination of the subscribers, who appoint scholars in rotation, according to the amount of their contributions to the charity. At the end of two years these boys are publicly examined for the Blue Coat School; after which, if their merit does not entitle them to one of the vacancies on the foundation, they remain in the Green School two years more; and are then dismissed at an age proper to be placed out in service. But if their progress has been such as to entitle them to a vacancy in the Blue Coat School, they are clothed and maintained there for two years, and at the expiration of that period, if they have made a competent progress in reading, writing, and accounts, and (in case the sea is their object) in navigation, they are placed out, with an apprentice fee of 3*l*. each, in husbandry, the sea service, or in some useful trade or occupation.

Upon the former plan, the funds of this charity provided in ten years, an education for seventy-five children: in the present mode,*

* Dr. Haygarth, who was the proposer of the *Green School,* suggested in 1797, a further improvement in it: that, in addition to their other learning, the greater part of the boys should alternately be instructed and employed in the needle manufacture, in a large unoccupied room, which is over the school. There is a want of occupation for boys at Chester, though there is already an established needle manufactory there, which might furnish employment, and finish the work. As to the Blue Coat boys, it was proposed that part

besides the increased motives for good behaviour and attention, three hundred and sixty-
two poor children of Chester receive an education during the same period. This has
been attended with no additional expense : the
degree of benefit, however far exceeds any
thing that could have been attained upon the
former system ; for the terms of succeeding to
the Blue Coat School, offered equally to all,
supplies that stimulating incentive to human
exertion, without which the best framed establishments lose their vital principle, and dege-
nerate into visionary and noxious theory.

Similar attention has been paid to the female
children in that town. It had been ascertained
by Dr. Haygarth, and some others, who were
in the habit of visiting the habitations of the
poor of Chester, that the girls there, as in many
other towns, were extremely destitute of useful
employment ; and that of those from nine to
thirteen years of age, in one parish, *three fourths*
could not sew at all, and not one of them so
well, as to make a single article of dress. They
were equally ignorant of knitting and spinning ;

of their profits should be laid up for their use and advancement in life, and those of the boys of the Green School paid
over to their parents.

and so unskilful in the common occupations of life, as to be disqualified for domestic servants, and for most other offices in society, and to have very few means of earning an honest livelihood.

It was calculated that four schools, of forty girls each, to be taught for four years, from the age of nine to thirteen years, in addition to a school already existing for maintaining and educating eight girls, would nearly provide for all the poor girls in Chester, who were unemployed, of a proper age for instruction, and in want of charitable aid for their education. It was therefore proposed that the girls should change their school every year, and (besides their being taught to read in all the schools, and attending the parish church twice on Sunday), that they should learn in the first year to knit, in the second to spin, in the third to sew, and in the fourth to wash and get up linen; the four schools being placed near the centre of the city, so that the scholars might, without inconvenience, go each year to a different school. In this manner it was calculated that, in the whole, the education of forty two girls would be annually completed.

The knitting, spinning, and sewing schools

had, from the time of their establishment in
1787, been regularly attended; and no difficulty had occurred in supplying work for the
knitters and spinners, though there had been
some at first, as to the sewing school. In procuring employment for the school for washing
and getting up linen, there has been very great
difficulty; and in consequence this part of the
plan was soon given up. The schools are now
reduced to two,* one for knitting, the other for
sewing; these are very well supplied with work,
and the children continue there for two years.

On their first appearance at school, the children come in but ill clothed, and not well behaved; but, in a short time, by their industry,
and by the co-operating benevolence of the
ladies who visit the school, they are not only
improved in behaviour, but are supplied with
uniform gowns and petticoats, as well as with
several other articles of dress; all their clothes,
except shoes and stockings, being made at the
sewing school.

* The great improvement of spinning mills has very nearly
deprived the poor of any profit by spinning. There are few
cottagers who have not suffered in this respect; but in some
parishes the labourers' wives and children are now entirely
precluded from this employment, without any other means of
occupation being opened to them.

The subscriptions were at first limited to five shillings each: though, among the more opulent, several persons of the same family were admitted as subscribers. They are at present not subject to limitation; and liberal donations have been made for supplying books, wheels, forms, and for other expenses. A considerable benefit has accrued from connecting these girl schools in some degree with the Sunday schools of Chester :—for, as an encouragement to good behaviour, the most deserving girls in the Sunday schools are regularly elected into the working schools. This has a powerful and extensive effect in improving the morals and behaviour of all the girls in the Sunday schools, and with them of almost all the female children in Chester.

It is not an unreasonable or unfounded presumption, that the extension of the schools at Chester will operate to improve the rising generation, in skill, industry, honesty, economy, sobriety, and in all those virtues, which result from a proper and religious education, and which can contribute to an useful and happy life.—There are very few of these virtues, that do not principally depend on education, and on the seeds sown in the mind during the early

period of life. A very able writer* has observed, that " drunkenness is the vice of an
uncultivated mind:" and in truth, with very few
exceptions, this vice, in all its beastly deformity, will be found to be most prevalent among
the ignorant and uninformed ; among those
who have had no means of improving or appreciating their faculties, and who, in respect
of mental and moral improvement, can be
placed but little above the brute creation.

In all those moral virtues, which are of such
inestimable value through life—of industry and
skill I say nothing, for it is obvious that instruction and habit are their vital principle—
but in moral virtues,—in fidelity, truth, justice,
and integrity,—every attainment is casual and
accidental,—all improvement, deceitful and
uncertain,—except that which originates in
principle, and whose basis firmly rests on the
sure ground of a religious education.

The absurd prejudices that *have* existed
against extending the common and general
benefits of education to the children of the
poor, and the extraordinary supposition, that
an uneducated and neglected boy will prove

* The Rev. Mr. Townsend in his Dissertation on the Poor
Laws.

an honest and useful man,—that a youth of
ignorance and idleness will produce a mature
age of industry and virtue,—are now in great
measure exploded. Switzerland and Scotland,
and the northern counties of England, where
the education and occupation of youth are particularly attended to, afford very gratifying
evidence of the contrary position. The individuals of those counties, are not only more industrious and more thriving, but, of all parts
of Europe, peculiarly exempt from criminal
habits.*

If the revenues of all our charity schools
were applied as advantageously as those of the
Blue Coat School, and the other schools at
Chester, it is probable that the funds would be
sufficient to give to every individual in England,
the same advantages of early instruction and
good habits, as are enjoyed by our northern
neighbours, and by the inhabitants of Switzerland. In order to produce this effect, some existing prejudices against removing ancient abuses,
and (I am sorry to be obliged to add) some degree
of interest or patronage in the continuance of
those abuses, must be given up; and the in-

---

* See Howard on Prisons, p. 124; and on Lazarettos,
p. 120.

quiry must be fairly and impartially entered into, how the good effects of every charity may be best attained, and most widely extended, without injustice to its original objects. There is hardly any charitable fund in England to which the example of Chester may not in some degree apply ; and by the application of which, children may not be enabled to acquire those early habits of life, without which *wealth* and *power* (and even *liberty* itself) are to the possessors of but little value ;—too frequently the source of ungoverned passions ; pernicious at the same time to other members of society, and destructive to the welfare and existence of the community.

No. XVIII.

LADIES COMMITTEE FOR THE FEMALE POOR,

AT the Meeting * of the " Society for bettering the Condition of the Poor," (March 1804),
the Committee directed an Address to be sent
to those Ladies who were Subscribers to their
funds, and to some others, proposing the formation of a LADIES COMMITTEE, FOR PRO-
MOTING THE EDUCATION AND EMPLOYMENT
OF THE FEMALE POOR.—The want of instruction, and the means of occupation, are causes
which have contributed fatally and extensively
to the prevalence of *profligacy* and *misery* among
the lower classes of females in England, and
have called for the union and co-operation of
the more elevated and enlightened of the sex,
for the correction of so general an evil.

The objects proposed for consideration, were
classed under three heads ; 1st, the forming of
similar Committees in provincial towns, and in
the metropolis :—2d, the promoting of the

* Reports No. CXIII.

moral and religious education of the Female Poor; and 3dly, the supplying of them with healthful domestic employment. The plan included the formation of a seminary for educating the unprovided daughters of clergymen, officers, and others, as teachers, and governesses, for private families and female boarding schools.

The establishment of such a seminary, at the same time that it constituted a very desirable and essential part of the general plan, did certainly create a considerable portion of its difficulty. With a view, therefore, to anticipate objection and facilitate arrangement, a suggestion of some hints, or rather an outline on the subject, was circulated with the other papers.

The Plan, as soon as it was arranged, was submitted to HER MAJESTY; who has been graciously pleased to approve it, and to command her name to be inserted as PATRONESS, and those of the PRINCESSES, as VICE PATRONESSES, of the institution. With this powerful advantage, and with the permission of the Ladies who compose the primary Committee, notice of this Institution has been ordered to be circulated, and to be inserted in some of the

public papers; and, the primary Committee
having been originally formed, and the first
arrangements made, with THE QUEEN's approbation, it has been established that no election
of a Member of the Ladies Committee, nor any
Rule or Regulation for their government, shall
be valid, until it has had HER MAJESTY's
sanction.

It may appear unnecessary to trouble the
reader with any remarks, on the *justice* and *propriety* of restoring to women those employments, which decency and moral fitness seem
to have exclusively marked for their own. To
men, the extended commerce and increased
manufactures, the unbounded enterprise and
unrivalled prosperity, of Britain will supply
countless occupations, adapted to every turn of
mind, and to every shade and gradation of
talent. At the present crisis, and probably
for some years to come, the strength and vigour
of every *male* arm will be wanted, for the de-
fence and protection of our beloved and envied
country. To *women* there can be opened, at
best, but a limited scope of action; and it is
for the benefit of all, looking to the increase of
the general fund, that they should not be precluded from contributing their portion of pro-

ductive industry. Not merely the husband, the father, and the brother, are interested in their possessing the means of employment, but the community at large, every member of society, must feel the benefit of so great an addition to national produce and moral virtue.

Is charity the object?—Reason and practical experience will demonstrate, that to enable even a few individuals to live by the exertions of industry, and to preserve them from vice and indigence, is an act of greater and more useful charity, than to feed thousands in gratuitous idleness. The operation is in itself more easy; and the effect once produced, the labour ceases, and only the pleasure and gratification remain.

These are general motives, applicable to every period and region of the world; but they must have tenfold weight in the British empire, at the present hour. A pestilential disease, of the most malignant nature, has corrupted the morals and mental sanity of a large portion of Europe. In order to exclude the infection, some line of demarcation is necessary to be drawn between Britain and the infected regions: and, if more cannot be done,—at least that sex, to whose early care and instruction, we owe the religious and virtuous impressions of the infantine and youthful age,* should be preserved pure and immacculate ; so as to be rendered the instruments of health and safety to others, whom curiosity or inattention may have exposed to the contagion.

If we will take the trouble to compare the moral and religious state of England with that of France and Italy, and to appreciate the *probable* character of masters imported from either of those countries, we may judge how far it can be wise and judicious, or even fit and decent, that the instruction of our daughters and sisters, in music, dancing, drawing, French,† and

* Where in mature life, men have surmounted great trials and temptations, it will almost always be found, that to the *early maternal lesson* they were indebted for their strength and preservation.

† Though it is *foreign* to the present subject, yet it is hardly possible to avoid noticing the many and great disadvantages, to which England has been subjected, by the FRENCH LANGUAGE having been adopted, as the general channel of communication, in all matters of *foreign treaty*.— Whilst this and other kingdoms in Europe have been negotiating in a foreign tongue, France has had the partial and unjust benefit of using her own idiom and her own dialect.—The aboriginal language of modern Europe is the Latin. If this, the dialect of ancient Rome, were to be generally used by the *diplomatic corps*, instead of French, more certainty and more justice would be obtained, by the usage of a dead and ascertained language, instead of a transient and fluctuating phraseology. —If the correction of this inconvenience be desirable and

the variety of crowded and incumbered accom-
plishments, which do now make essential parts
of female education in every rank and station
in life, should be intrusted to such adventurers,
—tinctured as many of them must be with foreign habits and vices ;—and this too, of young
women in the bloom of youth, at the period
when the female character is to formed, and
when every exertion ought to be made to fix
*the eternal and unvaried principles of religion and
virtue* indelibly on the mind. Those who have
had any opportunity of appreciating the superior degree of taste, talent, refinement of feeling, and sympathy of character, which many
English women possess, may correctly ascertain, whether they are by nature unfitted to
communicate instruction to their own sex, and
how far the employment of *foreign men*, for the
education of *English women*, is a necessary and
incorrigible evil.

practicable, it is hardly necessary to observe, that the present
is, of all times the most practicable, propitious, and favourable
to such an alteration.—As to the use of the French language
in female schools, it is impossible not to observe of many of
the sources of literature which it opens, that they are highly
tainted and infected. At the same time there seems to be but
little hope of succeeding, under modern prejudices, in bringing the language into any degree of disuse.

The personal attendance of *male* hair dressers, shoemakers, and staymakers, in the dressing rooms and private apartments of our fair countrywomen, has been frequently noticed, not only as indecorous, but as derogatory to the character and intrinsic purity of the sex. It should seem natural for female delicacy to accept, as an attendant at the toilet, the assistance of a virtuous and well educated English woman, in preference to *men*, unknown, unaccredited, and no otherwise recommended than by having been imported from the shores of France or Italy. It should also seem natural for ladies who feel what is due, either to their own character, or to the unprotected of their own sex, to desire to frequent those shops only, from whence the employment and assistance of women are not entirely excluded; and to avoid those, where files of athletic men,*

---

* In this age of chivalry and warlike enterprise, the appeal might with confidence be made to the *gallantry* and *bravery* of those gentlemen, who, so *bravely* and so *gallantly* equipped, do now attend, *in the place of females*, in many of the shops of the metropolis,—whether they will not be better employed in defending their fair countrywomen, than in depriving them of the means of support and existence ?—Whether they would not handle a Birmingham firelock better than Brussels lace ; and feel more satisfaction in pinning a Frenchman to the ground, than a feather to a cap ?—Admired as they now

ranged in order behind the counter, are employed, like Hercules in the service of Omphale, in the most minute, trivial, and effeminate occupations of the female sex.—

In the execution of the proposed plan, it is of great importance for those ladies, whose talents and discretion will direct the efforts of their benevolent coadjutors, to caution them not to attempt too many, or too extensive objects:—an attempt, which may excite the jealousy and hostility of some, who might otherwise have been disposed to have given not merely their wishes, but their aid, to the attainment of proper and practicable objects.—If, without carrying the war into the aggressor's country, the fair sex can only regain the territory which has been wrested from them,—or (to drop the metaphor) if, without interfering with any occupation which properly belongs to men, they can resume those which do peculiarly and exclusively appertain to their own sex,—those which public morals and female

justly are, whether they will not be more admired, when decorated with a military uniform, and employed in manly occupation? And whether the love and gratitude of the sex will not be more delightful, than the confidence of the toilet, or an occasional smile of approbation, on the tasteful disposition of a ribband?

decency require to be in the hands of women,
—and which the candour and good sense of
every unprejudiced man would admit to be
proper for women only ;—and if to this they
can add, for the benefit of the ignorant and unprotected of their own sex, such a degree of
education,* as may make them useful to themselves and to society, and may impress them
with the principles of religious and moral
truth,—MILLIONS, WHO MIGHT OTHERWISE
HAVE SUNK IN MISERY AND VICE, will live innocent and happy ;—will live to commemorate
the virtues, and record the names, of their
BENEFACTRESSES ;—as the friends, not only of
their country, but of the human race.

1*3th April,* 1804.

* One of the most important objects of the Ladies Committee will be to establish a seminary, for the education of
female teachers and governesses. In such a school it seems
to be indispensable that the establishment should be strictly
of the Church of England ; not from exclusive bigotry, operating to the prejudice of any denomination of Christians, but
from the necessity of the peculiar doctrines of every church,
making an essential part of education for teachers of youth :
—a consideration very often neglected in the selection of a
teacher, or governess.—Nothing will prevent the establishment of similar schools for other sects, and those even with
the assistance of the Ladies Committee, or at least some of
the District Committees. It will probably be found that of
all persuasions of Christians in England, those of the Established Church have been most deficient in the provision for the
peculiar education of their own poor.

No. XIX.

EDUCATION OF THE POOR IN IRELAND.

In the course of the benevolent exertions *
which have been made at Dublin, by the association for " discountenancing vice, and for
" promoting the knowledge and practice of
" religion and virtue," circular letters had
been sent to their own members, requesting
information upon the subject ; and other letters
have been since addressed to the Archbishops
and Bishops, soliciting, through their interference, returns from the parochial clergy to
queries, respecting not only the actual state of
education in their several parishes, but also as
to the impediments by which its progress is
obstructed, and the means whereby they might
be removed. The object of these enquiries
being to ascertain how far it may be expedient
for the public to interfere in removing these
impediments, and how far the suggestions or
exertions of individuals can be usefully directed

* Reports, No. CXVII.

to an object at present so very important to the country.

Parochial returns have been made from two hundred and two parishes; comprising about one-fifth of the ecclesiastical benefices in Ireland; and containing details which, while they may tend to gratify the reader, by shewing the great effects of some recent attempts to enlighten and improve the Irish poor, will operate to incite him to action, by pointing out *large districts where education is almost wholly neglected*, and will encourage exertion by the evidence which they afford, that there do not at present exist in Ireland any considerable obstacles, and certainly no insuperable difficulties, either religious or political, to a general system of education for the Irish poor.

The evidence to be collected from these Returns is, that *above two-third parts* of the poor children in Ireland, of an age, capacity, and disposition, to be taught and prepared for civilized life, are *entirely* without instruction or the means of education; that in certain parts of Ireland, anciently the most civilised and enlightened, the proportion of this moral and political evil is still greater; and that even in the very neighbourhood of some parishes, in which great and successful efforts have been recently made, for extending generally the benefits of virtuous and religious Institution, (such as New Ross, Whitechurch, and Carron) there do, at the present hour, exist parishes, which are comparatively speaking, without any means of education whatever.

The impediments to the instruction of the Irish poor, as appears by these Returns, are *the want of habitable school houses ;*—and (an obvious consequence) the *want of proper schoolmasters.* The instructors of youth, in those parts which supply them no certain income or habitation, form a peculiar species of *uncharactered itinerants;* who, in the winter barely subsist, by offering their services from house to house, and in summer, draw a scanty and precarious support, by wandering from parish to parish, and opening during the summer season, in some ditch covered with heath and furze, a school, to which the wretched inhabitants send their naked starving children, to learn reading, writing, and accounts.

Of other impediments, the principal seems to originate in *the poverty of the parents*, which not only prevents them from contributing to the weekly expense of schooling, but disables

them from supplying their children with clothing to attend the schools. *The want of proper
books* is another difficulty, prevailing to a degree, which we can form very little conception
of in this country ; whole parishes being stated
to be without a Bible,* or any other religious
book, in the houses, or in the schools of the
poor ; their place being supplied by " such
" romances and histories of profligate and dar-
" ing adventurers, as have been handed down
" from generation to generation, and must con-
" tribute to cherish an unsettled and irregular
" spirit, irreconcileable with the habits of order
" and industry."

In a country long inveterated in religious
prejudices, and recently convulsed by domestic
hostilities, commencing in distinctions of sects,
it is a most favourable circumstance to Christian charity, that there are to be found in the
returns of above two hundred parishes, very
few and imperfect traces of sectarism producing

* This return was prior to the exertions of the Dublin
Association for distributing Bibles and Testaments among the
poor of Ireland. In a note to the Introductory Letter to the
fourth Volume of the Reports, the reader will find notice of the
honourable and benevolent efforts, which the Association has
made in that respect. One can only regret that the imperious
magnitude of the call should be such, as to exceed even
these supplies from Christian benevolence.

impediments to education. In many parts the
Roman Catholic priests offer co-operation;
and it appears, that the children of Papists *
attend the Protestant schools without objection,
whenever education, not conversion, is the object. It also appears, that there are several
Catholic schools, where Protestant children
attend, and are instructed in the sacred Scrip-
tures, and in the Catechism of the Church of
England; that the New Testament is now read
in many of the Catholic schools, and that the
opinion is expressed, even in the most ignorant + and bigoted parts of the Western district of Ireland, that " if proper Protestant
masters were appointed, *and no works of con-*

---

* While charity, kindness, and mutual concession between
sects are recommended, it must not be omitted to caution
against that particular species of *religious candour*, which originates in *indifference* to every religious concern; and to
adopt the observation in these Returns, that in our endeavours
to promote harmony between sects, too much care cannot be
exerted to prevent the sacrifice of the VITAL PRINCIPLES
of religion itself.

+ With respect to the Latin language, formerly so prevalent in the western parts of Ireland, the fact is too curious to
be left unnoticed, that in the diocese of Limerick only one
Latin school is returned: all the remaining vestiges of Roman
literature being, it is stated, preserved by traditionary care,
in the *wilder and more mountainous parts* of the county of
Kerry.

" *troversy taught*, the children of Catholics
" would attend them."

This is to be accounted for by circumstances
which are repeatedly noticed in these Returns,
viz.—that the Irish poor, *at the present time*, are
extremely anxious that their children should
have the benefit of instruction ;—that a general
system of education would be *now* received by
the lower ranks with the warmest gratitude,
and would produce the most beneficial effects ;
—that if land were granted for that purpose,
many parishes would build houses for schoolmasters ;—and that in the opinion of the oldest
residents, *their wish for improvement never was*
SO STRONG *as at the present period.*

4 *June*, 1804.

No. XX.

EDUCATION OF THE POOR IN SCOTLAND.

By an act of the King (James VI.) and privy
Council of the 10th December, 1616, it was
recommended to the bishops to *deale* and *travel*
with the heritors, (land proprietors) and inhabitants of the several parishes in their respective dioceses, towards the fixing upon " some
" certain, solid, and sure course" for settling
and entertaining a school* in each parish.
This was ratified by a statute of Charles I. (in
the year 1633), which empowered the Bishop,
with the consent of the heritors of a parish, or
of a majority of the inhabitants, if the heritors
refused to attend the meeting, to assess every
plough of land (that is every farm in proportion to the number of ploughs upon it) with a
certain sum for establishing a school. This
was an ineffectual provision, as depending on
the consent and pleasure of the heritors and
inhabitants. Therefore a new order of things

* Reports, No. CXXVIII.

was introduced by an act passed in 1646, which obliges the heritors and minister of each parish to meet and assess the several heritors with the requisite sum for building a school house, and to elect a schoolmaster, and modify a salary for him in all time to come. The salary is ordered not to be under one hundred, nor above two hundred merks, that is, in our present sterling money, not under 5*l.* 11*s.* 1½*d.* nor above 11*l.* 2*s.* 3*d.* ; and the assessment is to be laid on the land, in the same proportion as it is rated for the support of the clergy, and as it regulates the payment of the land tax, But in case the heritors of any parish, or the majority of them, should fail to discharge this duty, then the persons forming what is called the Committee of Supply of the county, (consisting of the principal landholders), or any five of them, are authorized by the statute to impose the assessment instead of them, on the representation of the presbytery in which the parish is situated. To secure the choice of a proper teacher, the right of election of the heritors, by a statute passed in the year 1693, is made subject to the review and controul of the presbytery of the district ; who have the examination of the person proposed, committed to them, both as to his qualifications as a teacher, and as to his proper deportment in the office when settled in it. The election of the heritors is therefore only a presentment of a person, for the approbation of the presbytery : who, if they find him unfit, may declare his incapacity, and thus oblige them to elect anew.

The legal salary of the schoolmaster was not inconsiderable at the time it was fixed ; but by the decrease in the value of money, it is now certainly inadequate to its object; and it is painful to observe, that the landholders of Scotland resisted the humble application of the schoolmasters to the legislature for its increase a few years ago. The number of parishes in Scotland is 877 ; and if we allow the salary of a schoolmaster in each to be, on an average, seven pounds sterling,* the amount of the legal provision will be 6139*l.* sterling. If we suppose the wages paid by the scholars to amount to twice this sum, which is probably beyond the truth, the total of the expenses among 1,526,492 persons, (the whole population of Scotland,) of this most important establishment, will be 18,417*l.* But on this, as well as on

---

* This is now increased to more than double the former amount.—See p. 265.

other subjects respecting Scotland, accurate information may soon be expected from Sir John Sinclair's Analysis of his Statistics, which will complete the immortal monument he has reared to his patriotism.

The benefit arising in Scotland from the instruction of the poor, was soon felt; and by an act of the British parliament, 4 Geo. I. chap. vi. it is enacted, " that of the monies arising from the sale of the Scottish estates forfeited in the rebellion of 1715, 20,000*l.* sterling shall be converted into a capital stock, the interest of which shall be laid out in erecting and maintaining schools in the Highlands." The Society for promoting Christian Knowledge,* incorporated in 1709, have applied a large part of their fund for the same purpose. By their report, 1st May, 1795, the annual sum employed by them, in supporting their schools in the Highlands and Islands, was 3913*l.* 19*s.* 10*d.* in which are taught the English language,

---

* " The want" (says the judicious Hooker), " of the knowledge of God, is the cause of all iniquity amongst men, as contrariwise, the ground of all our happiness, and the seed of whatsoever perfect virtue groweth from us, is a right opinion touching things divine.—For the instruction therefore of all sorts of men to eternal life, it is necessary that the sacred and saving truths of God be openly published to them." 5. 8.

reading and writing, and the principles of religion. The schools of the Society are additional to the legal schools, which, from the great extent of many of the Highland parishes, were found insufficient. Besides these established schools, the lower classes of the people in Scotland, where the parishes are large, often combine together, and establish private schools of their own, at one of which it was that Burns received the principal part of his education. So convinced indeed are the poor people of Scotland, by experience, of the benefit of instruction to their children, that though they may often find it difficult to feed and clothe them, some kind of school instruction they almost always procure them.

1st May, 1800.

No. XXI.

SCOTCH LAWS RELATING TO EDUCATION.

AT a time when the public attention is directed
to the education of the poor, it will be useful to
ascertain what have been the measures, which have
so effectually given to Scotland those advantages of
moral and religious discipline, from which many
of the other parts of the Island continue to be excluded. We therefore add copies of those Scotch
laws, which in a very few years, brought many
thousands of dissolute and noxious poor into a
state of civil order, and made Scotland one of the
examples of the inestimable benefits which a system
of national instruction for the poor, confers on
morality and good government. These Acts will
shew how simple and unembarrassed the measures
might be, that would give the English poor and the
community these important advantages. The inducing the effectual co-operation of the endowments
and establishments for the instruction of the poor
already existing in this country, seems to be almost*

---

* Reports, Appendix to Vol. V.

the only object, which requires previous inquiry and investigation.

Act of Privy Council, 10th Dec. 1616.

FORASMUCH as the KING'S MAJESTY having a special care and regard that the true religion be advanced and established in all the parts of this kingdom, and that all his Majesty's sub-jects, especially the youth, be exercised and trained up in civility, godliness, knowledge, and learning; that the vulgar English tongue be universally planted, and the Irish language, which is one of the chief, and principal causes of the continuance of barbarity and incivility amongst the inhabitants of the Isles and High-lands, may be abolished and removed. And whereas there is no means more powerful to further this his Majesty's princely regard and purpose, than the establishing of schools in the particular parishes of his kingdom, where the youth may be taught at the least to write and to read,* and be catechised and in-structed in the grounds of religion: therefore the King's Majesty, with advice of the lords of

* There is a Scotch act of 1494, for promoting the edu-cation of the higher classes, and another of 1579, for instruc-tion of youth in the art of music. These I omit as not applying to the subject of the education of the poor.

his secret council, has thought it necessary and expedient, in every parish of this kingdom where convenient means may be had for entertaining a school, that a school shall be established, and a fit person appointed to teach the same, upon the expense of the parishioners, according to the quantity and quality of the parish, at the sight and by the advice of the Bishop of the diocese in his visitation: commanding hereby all the Bishops within this kingdom, that they and every one of them, within their several dioceses, deal and travel with the parishioners of their particular parishes within their said dioceses, to condescend and agree upon some certain, solid, and sure course, how, and by what means the said schools may be entertained: and if any difficulty shall arise amongst them concerning this matter, that the said Bishop report the same to the said lords, to the effect they may take such order thereabout as they shall think expedient: and that letters be directed to make publication hereof, that none pretend ignorance of the same.

Act of Parliament 1633, c. 5.

OUR SOVEREIGN LORD, with the advice of the states, ratifies the act of secret council dated at Edinburgh, the tenth day of December, one thousand six hundred and sixteen years, as to the planting of schools; with this addition, that the Bishops in their several visitations, shall have power, with consent of the renters and most part of the parishioners, and if the renters, being lawfully warned, refuse to appear, then with consent of the most part of the parishioners, to set down and stent upon every plough or husband land, according to the worth, for maintenance and establishing of the said schools. And if any person shall find himself grieved, it shall be lawful to him to have recourse to the lords of secret conncil, for redress of any prejudice he may or doth sustain. And he doth ordain letters to be directed for charging of the possessioners, to answer and obey the schoolmasters, of the duties that shall be appointed in manner aforesaid.

Act of Parliament, 1696, c. 26

OUR SOVEREIGN LORD, considering how prejudicial the want of schools in many places *

---

* The statute of 1696, (says Dr. CURRIE), the noble legacy of the Scottish Parliament to their country, began soon to operate; and happily, *as the minds of the poor received instruction,* the Union opened new channels of industry, and new fields of action to their view. In the year 1698, (I state this on the high and unquestioned authority of Mr. Fletcher of Saltoun) " there were in Scotland 200,000 people

have been, and how beneficial the establishing thereof in every parish will be to this church and kingdom ; therefore his Majesty with advice and consent of the estates * of Parliament, statutes and ordains, that there be a school settled and established, and a schoolmaster appointed in every parish, not already provided by advice of the heretors and ministers of the

" begging from door to door :—and at other times there had " not been less than 100,000 of these vagabonds, who lived " without any regard or subjection either to the laws of the " land, or even to those of God and nature;—frequently " guilty of robbery, and sometimes of murder ; — both men " and women, perpetually drunk, cursing, blaspheming, and " fighting together :" such however, in the course of a few passing years, was the effect of this Scotch Act for Education, that at the present day (as Dr. Currie observes), " there is no " country in Europe, in which, in proportion to its population, " so small a number of crimes fall under the chastisement of " the criminal law of Scotland."—In the Protestant cantons of Switzerland, and in New England, the peasantry have the same advantage of schools. This is also the case in certain districts of England, particularly in the northern parts of Yorkshire and of Lancashire, and in the counties of Westmorland and Cumberland. The peasantry of Westmorland (to continue a series of quotations from Dr. Currie), and of the other disticts mentioned before, if their physical and moral qualities be taken together, are superior to the peasantry in any other part of the island.

* Dr. Currie observes, that the same legislature which established a system of instruction for the poor, resisted the introduction of a legal provision for the support of poverty: and imputes to this circumstance, that the Scotch have a more than a usual share of prudence and reflection.

parish : and for that effect, that the heretors in every parish meet and provide a commodious house for a school, and settle and modify a salary to a schoolmaster, which shall not be under an hundred merks, nor above two hundred merks,* to be paid yearly at two terms, *Whitsunday* and *Martinmas*, by equal portions; and that they stent and lay on the said salary, conformably to every renter's valued rent within the parish; allowing each renter relief from his tenants of the half of his proportion, for settling and maintaining of a school and payment of the schoolmaster's salary;

* The lesser of these sums is 5*l*. 11*s*. 1½*d*., the greater 11*l*. 2*s*. 3*d*. By the 43d of George III. these salaries are not to be less than 16*l*. 13*s*. 4¼*d*. nor more than 22*l*. 4*s*. 6*d*. With the increase, however, it is still to be considered as an annual fee to engage their services, rather than as a compensation for the performance of them. While the salary establishes the school, the pay received from the scholars, though very small as to each individual, make up the amount of the master's income. By these means it becomes, not merely a consideration of interest, but in some degree a matter of necessity, for Scotch schoolmasters to attract scholars to the school; and I have been informed that the effects of this, in promoting and increasing the utility of the Scotch parochial schools have been very important Though the scholar's payment is only from six to twelve shillings a year, yet to a person who already has a school-house and salary, the addition of scholars makes a material addition to his income; while at the same time he finds that his school will never be beneficial to him unless it is made useful to the public.

which salary is declared to be by and attom the casualties, which formerly belonged to the readers and clerks of the Kirk session. And if the heretors or major part of them shall not convene, or being convened shall not agree among themselves, then, and in that case, the Presbytery shall apply to the Commissioners of the supply for the shire, who, or any five of them, shall have power to establish a school, and setttle and modify a salary for a schoolmaster, not being under one hundred merks, nor above two hundred merks yearly, as afore; and to stent and lay on the same upon the heretors conformably to their valued rent, which shall be as valid and effectual as if it had been done by the heretors themselves. And because the proportion imposed upon every heretor will be but small, therefore, for the better and more ready payment thereof, it is statuated and ordained, that if two terms proportions run in the third unpaid, then those that so fail in payment, shall be liable in the double of their proportions then resting, and in the double of every term's proportion that shall be resting thereafter, until the schoolmaster be completely paid; and that without any defalcation. And that letters of horning,

and all other executorials necessary be directed
at the instance of the schoolmaster, for payment
of the said stipend, and double of the proportions in manner aforesaid ; and discharges all
suspensions to pass against schoolmasters of the
salaries, except upon consignation or a valid
discharge : and if any suspension be past, that
the lords discuss the same summarily, without
abiding the course of the roll. And it is
hereby declared, that life renters, during the
lifetime, shall be liable in payment of the proportions imposed on the lands life rented ;
and execution, in manner foresaid, shall pass
against them for that effect ; and the heretors
shall be always free of the same during the
life renter's lifetime. And if any person find
themselves wronged by the inequality of the
proportions imposed, it shall be lawful for them
to seek redress thereof before the commissioners
of supply, sheriff of the shire, or other judge
competent, within the space of a year and a
day after the imposing of the stent, and no
otherwise. And also it is declared, that the
providing of the said schools and schoolmasters
is a pious * use within the parish, to which it

* There was a circumstance in the religious establishment
both of Scotland and New England, extremely favourable to

shall be lawful leisinne to patrons, to employ
the vacant stipends as they shall see cause ;
excepting from this act the bounds of the synod
of *Argyle:* in respect, that by a former act

these schools,—the co-operation of the parochial clergy.
The period preparatory to holy orders, was very generally
filled up by the exercise of the duties of the parish schoolmaster. This has many advantages.—It prepares the clergy
for those parochial functions, which they are going to sustain.
It gives consequence and consideration to these seminaries of
instruction, on account of the literary and respectable character of the masters thus acquired : and it affords a provision
for the scholar, in the interval between the period of his education and of his admission to the exercise of his religious
functions. It is thereby, in many instances, not only contri-
butory to the future usefulness and respectability of the clergyman, but it is convenient to his present pecuniary circumstances. These advantages are still further extended in Scotland, by that which exists only partially in the other parts of the
British empire; the constant residence of the parochial clergy.
" The clergyman," says Dr. Currie, " being every where resi-
" dent in his particular parish, becomes the natural patron
" and superintendant of the parish school; and is enabled in
" various ways to promote the comfort of the teacher, and
" the proficiency of the scholars. The teacher himself is
" often a candidate for holy orders, who, during the long
" course of study and probation required in the Scottish
" church, renders the time, which can be spared from his pro-
" fessional studies, useful to others as well as to himself, by
" assuming the respectable character of schoolmaster." Dr.
Beattie was educated at one of these parish schools; and on
his quitting the Marischall College at Aberdeen, was five years
schoolmaster of the little obscure parish of Ferdoun ; where
he continued his studies, and produced some of his most
beautiful poetical compositions.

of Parliament, in the year one thousand six hundred and ninety, the vacant stipends within the said bounds are destined for the setting up and maintaining of schools in manner therein mentioned: and the said vacant stipends are hereby expressly appointed to be thereto applied, at the sight of the sheriff of the bounds foresaid. And lastly, His Majesty with the advice and consent aforesaid, ratifies and approves all former laws, customs, and constitutions, made for establishing and maintaining of schools within the kingdom, in so far as the same are not altered nor innovate by this present act.

October 2, 1807.

No. XXII.

MASSACHUSETS ACT AS TO EDUCATION.

BE IT ENACTED,* That every town within this province, having the number of fifty house-holders or upwards, shall be constantly pro-vided of a schoolmaster, to teach children and youth to read and write. And where any town or towns have the number of one hundred families, or housholders, there shall also be a grammar school+ set up in every such town, and some discreet person of good conversation, well instructed in the tongues, procured to keep such school ; every such schoolmaster to be suitably encouraged and paid by the inhabi-tants.

* Reports, Appendix to Vol. III., this Act for the support of FREE SCHOOLS was passed in 1692.

† Many of these *free schools* were kept by young men, who had just taken their bachelor's degree, at Harvard College, and were looking forward to *holy orders;* filling up this interval with occupation, which, at the same time that it offered a supply towards the expense of their education, afforded not merely a preparation for the general object to which they were to be devoted, but a personal and practical knowledge of those persons, for whom, and for whose reli-gious instruction, they were to be ordained.

AND the select men and inhabitants of such towns respectively, shall take effectual care, and make due provision, for the settlement and maintenance of such schoolmaster and masters.

AND if any town, qualified as before expressed, shall neglect the due observance of this act, for the procuring and settling of any such schoolmaster as aforesaid, by the space of one year ; every such defective town shall incur the penalty of ten pounds for every conviction of such neglect, upon complaint made unto their Majesty's justices in quarter sessions for the same county, in which such defective town lieth ; which penalty shall be towards the support of such school or schools within the same county, where there may be most need, at the discretion of the justices in quarter sessions ; to be levied by warrant from the said court of sessions, in proportion, upon the inhabitants of such defective town, as other public charges, and to be paid unto the county treasurer.

No. XXIII.

REWARDS OF THE CHILDREN AT CAMPSALL SCHOOL.

The following rewards have been given to the Children attending at Campsall School, as an inducement to good conduct, and as the means of furnishing them with decent clothing and some useful books, during their continuance at the school, and upon their going into service.

1. EVERY * girl who comes to school, at or as near as may be, the time appointed ;—who has her hair, face, neck, and hands quite clean, and her clothes in good order and properly mended :—who takes pains to improve in reading, and whatever else she has an opportunity of learning ;—who performs her task in sewing, knitting, straw platt, &c. and does it as well as can reasonably be expected ;—and who does not in any respect behave ill :—will each day receive a white ticket, having marked on it No. 1, 2, 3, &c.

* Reports to Appendix, Vol. V.

2. On Sundays, and other days when the girls attend the school twice a day, they may if they behave well, obtain two of these tickets; one in the morning, and the other in the afternoon.

3. If a girl is certainly known by the ladies to steal, cheat, or use bad words, either in school, or out of school, or to misbehave at church, she will not only receive no ticket on the day on which she is so detected, but will also forfeit twelve of the tickets which she had before received.

4. When a girl has one hundred of these tickets (in regular order from one to an hundred) she must return them to her teacher; and she will receive, instead of them, a prize ticket, having on it these words, " Reward of Diligence " and good Behaviour," No. 1, 2, or 3, &c. Each of these tickets will entitle the owner (on continued good behaviour) to the following sums of money: which are to be given to her in necessary clothing, useful books, and a small proportion of money, when, with the approbation of the ladies, she either goes to service, or becomes an apprentice.

No.	s.	d.	No.	s.	d.	No.	s.	d.
1	-	1	0	6	-	3	6	11	-	6	0
2	-	1	6	7	-	4	0	12	-	6	6
3	-	2	0	8	-	4	6	13	-	7	0
4	-	2	6	9	-	5	0	14	-	7	6
5	-	3	0	10	-	5	6	15	-	8	0

5. There will be no higher prize than No. 15. Should any girl obtain any more than fifteen red tickets, each of the succeeding number will be of the same value as No. 15.

6. No prize ticket will be given for any number of white tickets, that is not a complete hundred. If a girl loses any of the hundred she has received, she must return to her teacher such numbers as she has remaining; but she will not receive, instead of them, a prize ticket, or be intitled to any reward.

7. If a girl leaves school with the approbation of the ladies, before she has completed her hundred, she must return the tickets she possesses; and if she has not lost any that she received, she will have, instead of them, a present in proportion to the number of her tickets, and to the **value** of the prize tickets, to which, had she been able to complete her hundred, she would have been entitled.

8. Should it ever happen that a girl behaves so ill as to be dismissed the school, or that she

leaves off attending without the approbation of the ladies, she will receive in clothing, all the money due to her for her sale work; but her tickets of every sort must be returned to the ladies, and they will all be forfeited.

9. Every year in the beginning of November, a day will be appointed, on which each girl's progress in reading, sewing, &c. during the preceding year will be examined; and no other business will that day be done in the school. The following rewards will be distributed to those who appear to deserve them: to those who have made suitable improvement in reading, spelling, and understanding the meaning of words, a book; in writing, and accounts, either a pencil, a pen knife, pens, paper, or a writing book, &c.—in plain work, knitting with common needles, and a hook, and straw platting, either a pincushion, a workbag, a housewife, a pair of scissars, a pocket, or a pair of mitts, &c. Prizes for the different performances will be provided as nearly as possible of the same value; and each girl will be allowed to make her own choice from those allotted to the particular exercise for which she claims a prize. To each girl who has obtained the three prizes, a ticket

will be given, entitling the owner to the sum of 2s. 6d. ; the money to be distributed in the same manner, as that arising from the prize tickets.

10. To shew clearly, what improvement in work a girl has made during the course of the year, she is to give on each examination day, a small specimen ; which will be preserved, and compared with what she produces on the succeeding examination days. For girls under eight years of age, the specimen is to consist of straw platt, of seaming, hemming, stitching, marking the initials of their own names, darning, and making a button hole. Specimens of writing must also be preserved, and a note specifying improvement in reading, spelling, &c. The scholars who have not attended a full year, will, on the day appointed, be examined along with the other scholars, as to their progress in every branch of their learning. If they produce as good specimens of work, and perform their other exercises as well as can reasonably be expected from the opportunities of improvement which they have had, they will be entitled to the different prizes, and to the annual ticket on the terms above mentioned.

11. As those girls who have attended the

school regularly for several years, and behaved well, may obtain a considerable sum of reward-money; and more, perhaps, than is quite necessary for them the first year they go to service, and as some girls who leave school, do not go to service, or become apprentices; a part of the reward-money will in such cases, be retained by the ladies, and given to them on their marriage, or when they seem most to need it. If they continue to behave well they will be allowed five per cent interest for it. Should they not receive the whole of their reward money, before they attain the age of twenty-one, they may then dispose of the remaining part, in what manner they think proper.

12. Every girl who can read the prayer book, and knows how to make a proper use of it at church, will have one given to her by the ladies; or if she has one already, she will receive from them a present of some other book, about the same price.

13. The day before the anniversary of the Campsall Female Friendly Society, a straw bonnet and a coloured neck-handkerchief, will be given to every girl who has been diligent, earned as much as could reasonably be expected,

and taken care of the clothes she has received during the preceding year. The same present will be made to all the new scholars as an encouragement to them to behave well.

10*th April,* 1805.

No. XXIV.

COPY OF THE REGULATIONS OF THE SCHOOLS
OF ST. JOHN'S CHAPEL, BEDFORD ROW.

General Rules.

1. T H E * *support* of these schools is by annual
sermons only.

2. The *instruction* of the scholars is committed to such gentlemen and ladies, usually
attending this chapel, as are approved of by
the ministers, and are nominated by them to
be superintendants of the scholars; which
superintendants are assisted by a master and
mistress.

3. The *government* of the schools is vested in
the ministers, chapel wardens, and gentlemen
superintendants; who hold a meeting at the
vestry, the last Tuesday evening in every
month, at six o'clock, to regulate all matters
connected therewith.

4. The children who apply for admission

* These Regulations have not been published in the Society's
Reports, but are now first printed with permission of the Rev.
Mr. Cecil.

must be able to read ; and those are preferred, whose parents, or nearest relatives, usually attend this chapel.

5. Children are admitted into the schools at those monthly meetings, held on the last Tuesday in March, June, September, and December.

6. An annual sermon is preached to the scholars on May-day ; after which a meeting is held of the ministers, chapel wardens, and superintendants, when books are given to the scholars, of a value proportioned to their good behaviour during the year, and adapted to their age and capacity.

7. Besides these annual rewards, *Cheap Repository and other small Tracts*, of the value of five shillings, are provided annually for each superintendant. to be given as *occasional rewards among the deserving scholars.* As they pass through the schools, they are furnished with proper Catechisms, and a Prayer Book, and, if they behave well and improve, with a Psalm Book, and a Bible ; and, when they leave the schools, if they do it with credit to themselves, a larger Prayer Book and Bible are presented to them.

Rules for the Superintendents.

1. THEY engage to attend every Sunday morning *punctually at ten o'clock;* or, in case of unavoidable absence, either to provide a proper substitute for that morning, or to send notice the day before to the messenger, that such a substitute may be provided by the ministers.

2. They are requested to bring forward the scholars committed to their care, according to the age and capacity of such scholars, in the following system of religious instruction:— The Collects for the day: the Texts of the Sermons heard on the preceding Sunday: Dr. Watt's Divine Songs for Children: the Church Catechism: the Church Catechism broken into short Questions: and Stillingfleet's Explanation of the Church Catechism—and they are farther desired to explain to the scholars, and impress upon them, the truths of Christianity.

3. To every scholar who shall attend punctually in time, and repeat well the lessons of the morning, a printed certificate of approbation is given, a number of which are kept in the vestry for that purpose; and this certificate is to be marked, or numbered by the

superintendant, in such manner, as may be thought necessary to prevent deception.

4 The superintendants are desired to *propose Psalm Books and Bibles to those scholars who may not have received them, as rewards for their diligence;* and to make a report in writing to every monthly meeting of such scholars as have merited them. They are farther desired to engage the attention and care of the scholars by *occasional presents of Cheap Repository and other small Tracts, a proper selection of which,* of the value of five shillings, will be annually delivered to each superintendant *for that purpose*

5. They are empowered to suspend any scholar, for misdemeanors, from all connection with the schools, till the next monthly meeting; to which they are to report the cause of such suspension ; when the case is to be heard and determined.

6. They are desired to begin with the scholars punctually at *ten* o'clock, and to leave them at *ten minutes before eleven.*

7. When any scholar is absent two Sundays together, without a satisfactory reason being assigned, the superintendant is requested to send the messenger to inquire the occasion of such absence.

Rules for the Master and Mistress.

1. THEY are to instruct all such children as are not classed under any of the superintendents, and they have the same powers and duties with regard to such children, as are assigned to the superintendents over theirs.

2. They are to collect the scholars together; to keep accurate lists of them; and to regulate their behaviour during divine service.

3. They may suspend any scholar for misconduct, after the school hours; reporting the cause of such suspension to the next monthly meeting.

4. They are to employ such persons, with the approbation of any monthly meeting, as may be found requisite to assist in keeping perfect order and silence in the scholars' galleries, during divine service.

5. They are to be at the chapel *a quarter of* an hour before ten every Sunday morning, and *a quarter of* an hour before service begins in the afternoon and evening.

Rules for the Parents.

1. THE children are to be brought for admission by their parents or friends; and no

child is to be admitted. unless such parents or friends will engage for their good behaviour and punctual attendance.

2. Notice of the indisposition, or absence from town, of any scholar, is to be given by the parents or friends, to the messenger, that it may be reported by him to the superintendent of such scholar's class.

3. When a scholar has been suspended for misdemeanors, the parents or friends are to have notice of the cause, and are expected to accompany such scholar to the next monthly meeting, when the matter will be considered and determined.

4. They are expected to give notice to the monthly meeting, when any scholar is to leave the schools.

Rules for the Scholars.

1. Each scholar is to attend divine worship every Sunday morning, afternoon, and evening, unless a sufficient reason can be given for absence.

2. All are to be in their proper places before ten every Sunday morning, and before the bell shall cease to ring in the afternoon and evening.

3. Silence and reverence must be observed every moment they are in the house of God. There must be no whispering, talking, nor disturbance of any kind. Every little noise in the scholars' gallery disturbs the congregation in the gallery below. The first offence is punished by the forfeiture of all the tickets of approbation which the scholar may have then received. The second offence is punished by expulsion from the schools.

4. Each scholar is expected to come straight from home to the chapel, and to go directly home after divine service is ended, with quietness and good behaviour. All playing and rudeness in the streets on a Sunday, is disgraceful and sinful. The first offence is punished by the forfeiture of all the tickets of approbation the scholar may have then received, and for the second offence the punishment is expulsion.

5. *Boys* and *girls* are never to be seen walking together on a Sunday to or from the chapel.

6. They are expected to pay cheerful and constant obedience to the superintendants, master and mistress, and such persons as the master and mistress may appoint to assist in keeping order and silence in their galleries.

No. XXV.

ADDRESS TO PARENTS OF CHILDREN IN THE
SCHOOLS OF ST. JOHN'S CHAPEL, BEDFORD ROW.

W H E N * our Lord put the question, *What
shall it profit a man if he shall gain the whole
world, and lose his own soul?* He shewed the
infinite worth of that soul, and also the awful
consequences of neglecting it.

To make this more plain, he has given us a
book, shewing us in a variety of ways, that the
soul, like the body, has its *wants, diseases,* and
death, also its means of recovery to spiritual
health and eternal *life.*

This recovery is compared in Scripture to
the bringing *a lost sheep back again to the fold;*
or to one awaking from *a deadly sleep to a
lively hope:* as it is written, *Awake thou that
sleepest, and arise from the dead; and Christ shall
give thee light.*

Now RELIGIOUS INSTRUCTION is one of
God's appointed means for this relief and re-

* Now first printed by the Society, with Mr. Cecil's permission.

covery of the soul of man, as He saith, *Take fast hold of instruction; let it not go; keep it, for it is thy life.*

More particularly with respect to our children, He says, *Train up a child in the way he should go, and when he is old, he will not depart from it.* And accordingly he charges us, *In the morning to sow the seed of instruction, and in the evening not to withhold our hand, since we know not which shall prosper.*

A brutish man knoweth not, and a fool doth not understand this wisdom ; and therefore despiseth it. But mark what honour the Lord putteth upon it, when he saith, *Shall I hide from Abraham the thing that I do? For I know him, that he will command his children and his household after him to keep the way of the Lord.—Them that honour me I will honour.*

And because religious instruction is God's usual method of delivering us from the *blindness* of ignorance, and the *poison* of sin, He hath not only sent His word, and promised His spirit to them that ask Him ; but He has also raised up ministers and witnesses from time to time *to open men's eyes, to turn them from darkness to light, and from the power of Satan to God; that they may receive forgiveness of sins, and an inheritance among them that are sanctified by faith which is in Jesus.*

But that religious instruction which is needful at all times, is particularly needful in a day of rebuke and blasphemy, like the present. A sort of madness now abounds that leads guilty, dying creatures not only to ridicule and reject both the physicians, and the remedies God hath sent to heal them, but also to delight in spreading the pestilential disorder.

Now if some cruel wretch were contriving to give your child a dose of poison under the notion of a sweetmeat, could you rest till the child was informed of the danger, and secured against it? Or if the plague were to break out among us, would you be easy till the best remedies were administered to your family, and every thing tried for their safety?

What then are we to think of those who are so anxious to secure the *body* of a child which must soon turn to dust, and yet slight the means God has appointed for the safety of its never-dying *soul?*

None will need to have these things urged upon their consciences the moment after they enter eternity. But, few consider enough how

much, even in the *present* world, the comfort
of the parent depends upon the religious instruction of his child.

How many who have sowed the seed of religious instruction, are reaping the fruit of
their labours in the piety, affection, and prosperity of their children? On the other hand,
what fruitless complaining and bewailing is
often heard over a profligate son, or a ruined
daughter? And what bitter reflections must
follow in the mind of those parents who trace
this ruin from their own neglect?

I will judge, said the Lord, *the house of Eli
for ever, because his sons made themselves vile,
and he restrained them not.*

Consider the advantages of preparing your
children against the time they must leave you,
to struggle with a dangerous world. Good
principles form a suit of *armour.* They are
also a *recommendation;* for who would not prefer a servant, or a partner, who has been
brought up in the fear of God and the knowledge of his duty, to one who has been left to
run wild, neither fearing God, nor regarding
man?

Consider also, if they should be taken from

you by death, how painful will be the reflection, if they meet it in ignorance and unbelief, through your neglect? On the contrary, what a consolation it will be in parting with them, if, through God's blessing on your religious instructions you have ground to hope they are gone to Him?

Now, when to these considerations you add, that youth is the spring time to plant good principles, before bad ones take root: and how much easier it is to prevent evils than to cure them; we trust that those who have a *real* regard to the honour of God—to the souls and bodies of their children—and to their own future peace and comfort, will embrace and further the pious design of their friends, whose only object, in their expence and labour, is to make you and your children happy in time and in eternity.

To attain this end, we would begin by setting before your children their fallen and depraved state by nature, and the root of those evil tempers and practices by which they so dishonour God, distress you, and plunge themselves in destruction. We would teach them the nature of right and wrong, from the only infallible standard, God's holy law; a law *by which every mouth must be stopped, and all the world become guilty before God.*

After shewing them their ruin by sin, we would teach them their remedy in the Gospel, setting before them the necessity of *repentance towards God, and faith in our Lord Jesus Christ,* — the merit of his blood—the influence of his Spirit—and the obligations to a holy life and conversation.

But while we as their *friends* are using our endeavours, how much stronger reasons have you as their *parents* to join us in bringing them, as you are able, to the knowledge of God and themselves!—Leading your little ones (like those mentioned in the Gospel, *Mark* x. 13.) by faith and prayer to Christ, that He may take them into His arms and bless them.

There are, indeed, parents so vain and un-thinking, that they would be better pleased if their children were presented with baubles, articles of dress, money, &c. than with good books and religious instructions. On the con-trary, your friends have far nobler views;—they are seeking to adorn and enrich your children with those substantial benefits which can never be taken away from them.

You have already given good reason to hope that this also is your wish, from the great number of children who attend, and seem desirous of improvement in the best knowledge; and this hope will be greatly increased in proportion as you regard the following advice:

1. Shew them the nature and excellency of our design.

2. Strictly enjoin them to be exact in attending at the appointed times, and to be attentive to the instructions given them.

3. Give them admonitions and directions at home as to their behaviour in church, and in going thither and returning.

4. Encourage them to learn at home, what they will be expected to repeat at church; and inquire at home what they have heard at church, and explain to them what may be too difficult for their present capacity.

5. Keep them, by all means in your power, from loose and vicious books and companions; and endeavour to correct evil dispositions, before they take root, and resist all your efforts.

6. Frequently explain to them, and enforce upon their consciences, their ruined state by nature and practice—their redemption through Jesus Christ—and the necessity of the

Holy Spirit's influence to make them see and feel these truths.

7. Enjoin upon them regularity in private prayer, and reading the word of God.

8. Pray for a blessing on your and our endeavours; *for neither is he that planteth any thing, nor he that watereth, but* God *that giveth the increase.*

9. Be watchful over your own conduct, that your example may not counteract our instructions.

10. Despair of nothing in a right way, and with the Divine blessing: *Be not weary in well-doing; for, in due season, ye shall reap, if ye faint not.*

No. XXVI.

ADVICE TO THE FOUNDLING CHILDREN.

The following is a Copy of the Instructions,* which, with the signatures of the Governors present, are given to each of those Children of the Foundling Hospital in London, intitled to Rewards for good Conduct, when they attend the Committee to receive their Rewards, at the expiration of their Apprenticeships.

As the recompence for a long period of care and attention to your maintenance, education, and introduction into life, we have now the pleasing and enviable satisfaction of beholding you entering upon your course in this world, with many very important advantages ;—with a *character* to preserve,—with the *means of supporting* yourself by your own industry,—and with *instruction and habits of life*, so to direct your conduct in your present state of existence here, as to preserve the good name and reputation

* Reports, Appendix to Vol. IV.

which you have happily obtained, and to lay up for yourself a treasure of eternal and unfailing reward hereafter.

Few, if any, situations of life could be pointed out, so forlorn, so helpless, or so destitute of hope, as was yours, when, by the gracious intervention of Providence, the hospitable doors of this house were opened for your reception. Without a parent capable of supporting you, without a protector to whom your infant steps might be directed, you would have protracted your existence in a state of ignorance and beggary, or (an event much more probable) you must have perished in your infancy.

The directors and supporters of this charity received you.— You were adopted, by baptism, into the church of CHRIST; and you were then placed, under a careful inspector, in the country ; where your health and situation were frequently and anxiously examined and reported upon, and where every cause of disease and infirmity (so far at least as human care can provide) was removed, or prevented,

At the age of four or five years, when your faculties had so far advanced towards maturity as to be fitted for instruction, you were returned to these walls. The care of your religious and moral education, under the watchful eye of the governors, was then committed to instructors, whose *kindness* and *attention* do now, and we trust ever will, impress your mind with *affection* and *gratitude*.—Happy will it be for the children of the poor in this country, when the advantages of a similar education shall be extended to *all* of them:—and most unhappy, and most ungrateful, will you prove, if, with those advantages, you do not bring forth the genuine fruits of Christian education,—PIETY, —VIRTUE,—and INDUSTRY.

When your progress of instruction, and your period of life, had fitted you to be placed out as an apprentice, a proper situation was carefully sought for you; where the good habits, and untainted principles, of your early years might be confirmed and extended. From that to the present time, the provident care of your benefactors has been rather increased than diminished. Frequent investigations with regard to your conduct and situation, and constant and unwearied attention, on their part to guard against any circumstance which might blight or disappoint your hopes and expectations in life, have conducted you safely through the period of your apprenticeship.

You do *now* attend to receive that REWARD for your good conduct, and that TESTIMONIAL of it under the seal of this Corporation, which the governors are persuaded you are intitled to, not merely from the certificate of your master or mistress, but from their own knowledge of your conduct and behaviour, during the period of your apprenticeship. The bestowing, however, of that reward, and the signing of that testimonial, would afford but a small and imperfect mark of the interest which they take in your welfare, without the addition of ADVICE and INSTRUCTION, with regard to your future conduct through this world, to a happier and more perfect state of existence.

It should be your FIRST OBJECT in life, to have *a conscience void of offence towards* GOD, *and towards man;*—your second, *to maintain and support yourself* by your own industry and exertions; and to preserve, by *decency, civility,* and *propriety of behaviour,* that unblemished character, which you are, at present, so fortunate as to possess.

As to your primary and *your pre-eminent duty,* we exhort your always to bear in mind, that, in this world of trial, if GOD be for us, we need not mind what *man* shall say, or attempt to do, against us.—If HE is our protector, we may pass with security and peace through the valley of the shadow of death, and through every scene of danger or difficulty. If, on the contrary, HE casts us off, we have no other power to look to for succour and protection. To HIM, therefore, address yourself, *in fervent and frequent prayer*, not only in the church, but in your chamber; and look to him with *faith*, knowing that his mercy never was withheld from those, who sought him with piety and humility, and who relied on his protection.

If you are duly impressed with your duty to GOD, you will never fail in the performance of your duty to your *neighbour*. He who loveth God, will love his *brother* also:—and he who is obedient to the divine commands, will possess HONESTY, SOBRIETY, INDUSTRY, PRUDENCE, KINDNESS and FORBEARANCE; virtues, which are not only essential to your duty to GOD and to your *neighbour*,—but, as we shall endeavour to explain to you, of the most important and immediate consequence to your present welfare here, as well as to your eternal happiness hereafter.

Without HONESTY, which includes a strict adherence to TRUTH, you must not only relinquish the hope of thriving and being successful in your station of life, but you must look forward to *disgrace* and *punishment*, and probably to an ignominious end —THE MOST ABANDONED VILLAIN NEVER BEGAN HIS CAREER WITH ATROCIOUS CRIMES.—It is from petty and uncorrected habits of pilfering and falsehood,—it is from allowing our wandering desires to covet some little portion of our neighbour's goods,—and then attempting to avoid detection by falsehood or prevarication,—that the foundation of principle in the human heart is corrupted and undermined,—the impression of religious and moral habits gradually effaced, —and the hardened and abandoned criminal, at length, left to expiate, *by a public and ignominious death*, the crimes which he has perpetrated against his fellow creatures.

The blessing of *honesty* (like that of every other virtue) returns with accumulated advantage to the possessor : the influence, however, is directed in its more immediate effect, to others.—SOBRIETY, the virtue which we have next to observe upon, is an act of *self preservation;* and looks almost exclusively to our

own health and happiness. In its more enlarged sense, it includes an *abstinence from every
personal irregularity of conduct;* and, among
other irregularities, from that, against which,
with your early instruction and subsequent
habits, we trust it will be unnecessary to for-
warn you. We mean that vice, which in
young men leads them into improper and
criminal connections, and in women is generally
attended with every species of degraded and
prostituted * depravity. Of the victims of un-
regulated passions, you will find a melancholy
list in the annals of Newgate, and you will see
many wretched females in the public streets.
Happily for you, we repeat, with early religious instruction, and with subsequent care

* The preserving and educating of so many children, which
without the Foundling Hospital would have been lost to that
society of which they are calculated to become useful members, is certainly a great and public benefit. The adoption of
an helpless unprotected infant, the watching over its progress
to maturity, and the fitting it to be useful to itself and others
here, and to attain eternal happiness hereafter,—these are no
common or ordinary acts of beneficence;—but their value
and their importance are lost, when compared with the benefits
which (without any prejudice to the original objects of the
charity) the mothers derive from this Institution as it is at
present conducted. The preserving the mere vital functions
of an infant, cannot be put in competition with saving from
vice, misery, and infamy, a young woman, in the bloom of

and good habits, you have hitherto been preserved, through a period, when youth and in-
experience are most endangered.—May the
DIVINE MERCY still preserve and protect
you!

In its limited sense, SOBRIETY means an
abstinence from the intemperate use of spiri-
tous liquors.—From the miserable and disgusting examples, which this great metropolis
affords, let us warn you—and let us intreat
you—to avoid with abhorrence, the destructive
and abominable sin of *dram drinking.* Every
indulgence in this vice,—however trivial, however venial, such indulgence may appear *at first,*
—leads, through hopeless misery, to the gates
of death.—That which commenced in accident,
or in thoughtlessness, is soon confirmed by
habit, and called for by the cravings of disease.

life, whose crime may have been a *single* and solitary act of
indiscretion. Many extraordinary cases of repentance, followed by restoration to peace, comfort, and reputation, have
come within the knowledge of the writer of this note. Some
cases have occurred, within his observation, of wives happily
placed, the mothers of thriving families, who, but for the
saving aid of this Institution, might have become the most
noxious and abandoned prostitutes. Very rare are the instances,—none has come within notice,—of a woman relieved
by the Foundling Hospital, and not thereby preserved from
a course of prostitution,—B. 31*st Dec.* 1803.

The wretched victim feels no relief, but from the increase of the poisonous draught; and sinks by painful but hastened steps to his grave, —with this melancholy truth inscribed on his mind, if any religious impression yet remains, that *the drunkard shall not inherit the kingdom of* GOD.

From these destructive vices, it will be some relief to direct your attention to the delightful effects of INDUSTRY, and of those kindred virtues, on which we shall have next to observe. —If you are *industrious*, you will be useful to yourself,—to your friends,—to the community at large:—you will escape the seduction of bad company;—you will avoid many temptations, to which the idle and unoccupied are necessarily subjected. Instead of being a burthen and incumbrance to others, you will, by your diligence, not only obtain a provision for yourself and for your own immediate connections,— but you may be enabled (as you ought to do, if in your power) to set apart, every week, something for the relief and comfort of the unfortunate and necessitous.

It has been observed, that *vices* are seldom found single; but that VIRTUES go always together. They are social, not solitary, in their

nature. *Honesty, sobriety,* and *industry,* excellent and praiseworthy as they are, appear but
with diminished lustre, unless accompanied
by their sister virtue—PRUDENCE. To enable
you to reap and enjoy the fruits of your exertions, *prospective prudence,* which regards future
welfare and satisfaction in preference to present
indulgence and gratification, must direct your
conduct. Without it, your other good qualities will fail of the object of attainment.—
In some foreign countries, where the power
of the few, or the violence of the many, destroys
the security of property, the industrious have
but little encouragement to lay up the produce
of their labour. But in our own free and well
regulated government, the law holds out equal
and certain protection to all: every individual
is secured in the enjoyment of the fruits of his
own diligence and application.—Those, whom
we see in the possession of wealth and affluence,
are not exclusively, nor even the greater part
of them, persons who derive their fortunes from
their ancestors. They have mostly acquired
them by their own industry. And, where the
case is otherwise (whatever may have been accumulated by careful and thriving parents) if
their children are thoughtless, idle, and extra-

vagant, riches will soon make them wings, and
fly away.—Look to the acting Governors of this
GREAT AND USEFUL CHARITY, under whose
protection you have securely passed the preceding period of your life. You will find that
most of them owe their affluence and indepen-
dence to their own exertions and attentions.
As to many of them (for some we can speak
from self-experience) powerful facts may be
stated, in confirmation of our assertion, and as
inducements and incentives to your industry
and application.—It may be enough to remind
you, that, with the blessing of GOD, you
may, by attention and prudence, make the
same use as they have done of the advan
tages, which a good education has afforded
you.

With regard to KINDNESS and FORBEARANCE,
it is your duty to reflect, that, to the *benevolence* of those who first received you into this
House, you owe the comforts and advantages,
which you at present possess ; and that to the
MERCY OF GOD, and to that alone, you must
look for all your future hopes and happiness,
—here, and hereafter.—It will therefore, we
hope, be unnecessary to impress on your mind
(instructed as you have been in the principles

of our religion) the CHRISTIAN DUTY of culti-
vating these amiable and excellent virtues,—
and of forgiving, as you hope to be forgiven. We
shall therefore conclude, by intreating you to
be PIOUS AND HUMBLE,—to be HONEST, SOBER,
INDUSTRIOUS, PRUDENT, KIND HEARTED, AND
FORBEARING.—These are the qualities, by
which we call on you, to testify your gratitude
to your benefactors.—PROSPER, THRIVE, AND
BE USEFUL IN THE WORLD.—BE VIRTUCUS.
—BE HAPPY.—And we shall thereby receive
an abundant reward for every care and attention, which we have bestowed upon you.

27th April, 1803.

No. XXVII.

PROPOSED INQUIRY AS TO SCHOOLS.

In order * to the extension of a general system of religious and moral education among the poor, it is submitted that a previous Inquiry into the present state of charity and other schools will be requisite, in order to ascertain,

1. The places in which those schools are entirely adequate to the object ;

2. The places where a greater extension of their benefits is wanted, and such extension is practicable ; and

3. Those where new schools for the poor are necessary or expedient.

For this purpose it is proposed, that (with exception of the great classical schools, and of private seminaries receiving no support from charitable foundation, public aid, or private subscription) a parliamentary return be made from all the charity schools † in the kingdom, under the following heads :

* Reports, Appendix to Vol. IV.

† This would make a valuable supplement to the returns very recently made under Mr. Rose's Act, 43d George III.

1. The nature and amount of their respective income, annual or contingent, and arising from fines or otherwise, for five years last past.

2. The average number of children educated in each of the said schools during the five last years ; specifying the number of those children which have been clothed, and those which have been not only clothed but boarded.

3. The dates of the respective foundations of such schools ; and by whom, or in what manner, they were established.

4. The will, deed, or other regulation, by

—We find by those returns, comprising very nearly the whole of England and Wales, that the number of children (*out of the workhouse)* between five years and fourteen years of age, who have been the subject of *parish relief,* is 188,794; whereas the number of those, who have had the benefit of *schools of industry* and receiving education, have amounted only to 20,336 ; being not so much as one-ninth of the number receiving parish relief.—The poor's rate actually returned for one year, ending Easter 1803, considerably exceeds FIVE MILLIONS STERLING. Of this it appears by the returns, that only the sum of 10,927*l.* 6*s.* 6*d.* has been expended in materials for employing the poor out of the workhouse ; and 38,760*l.* 18*s.* 2*d.* in materials for employing them in the workhouse or house of industry ; two sums, which do not together amount to ONE HUNDREDTH PART of the money actually raised. The earnings of all the poor, in and out of the workhouse, amount to 87,272*l.* 10*s.* ; or about one-sixtieth of the money raised for them.—4 June, 1804.

which they are governed, and where deposited, proved, or registered.

5. Whether any, or what, practicable improvement, or extension, can be safely and properly adopted, as to the beneficial effects of their respetive schools.

This return may be made to the Clerk of the House of Commons: but it is conceived, that it would be better that it should be made to the Privy Council; and that the arrangement and application of the evidence to be obtained, and the report upon it, should be prepared by, or under the direction of a Special Committee of the Privy Council. The object of the report would be to point out any measures proper to be adopted for extending, either by the existing means. or by additional establishments, a proper and useful system of education for the benefit of all the lower classes.

The education of all the children of the poor may, it is conceived, be provided for ;

1. By opening the charity schools, or those established on charitable foundation, to all the original objects of the founder.

2. By engrafting on them day schools for the admission of all the other poor children of

the vicinage, on limited terms ; such as those adopted in West-street, Seven Dials, of three-pence per week, or in Chester.

3. By opening parochial schools (where wanted) for admission of the children of the poor, on terms of similar limitation.

4. By official application to the Lord Chan-cellor, where uncorrected abuses of charity schools are continued.

5. By enabling the magistrate (in certain cases and ages, when the parent is not able to pay the three-pence a week for his child's schooling) to order the payment of it, as an act of parish relief.

The whole system of education in this coun-try may be thus completed with a trifling alter-ation of the mode, and with very little if any increase in the parochial charges.

10th Jan. 1804.

No. XXVIII.

The History of Betty Thomson, and her Family and Neighbours; being the First Part of a practical Commentary on the Reports of the Society for bettering the Condition of the Poor.

CHAPTER I.

The Death of Squire Goodenough.—*Some Account of Him.—His grand Monument.— Who Mrs. Jones was.*

Squire Goodenough's death * last winter was regretted by every one ; but by none more, than by his tenants and neighbours at *Monk Appleton,* where his estate was situated, and where he had spent the last ten years of his life. The Squire, in his youth, had been called to the bar, and had had some share of business ; being a man of a sound understanding, and unsullied character, though not gifted

---

* This little narrative will not be found in the Reports, but is now first published. It is also printed separately for Distribution, in the hope of its inducing the Cottager to benefit by some of the improvements recommended by the Society.

with those peculiar talents, which are essential
to an elevated situation in that profession. His
age was between forty and fifty, when he came
into possession of his uncle's estate, on the
death of his cousin, without issue.

He determined to quit the law, to which he
had never been much attached; to put the
family seat in repair, and fixing himself in the
midst of his estate, to try how far the property
which had devolved to him upon his cousin's
death, could be made the source of comfort
and advantage to himself, and to those about
him. The greater part of his law library he
sold: and purchased all the Tracts he could
meet with, respecting the economy of the Poor,
and the improvement of their domestic habits
and comforts. He soon became capable of dis-
tinguishing between the different classes of au-
thors; between those who formed books from
the *day-dreams* of their waking hours, and those
who gave the result of what had been fairly
tried, and the observations which had occurred
during the trial.

Mr. Goodenough began by serving in rotation the different parish offices. He then took
out his *dedimus*, as a magistate. In his new
line of the profession, he found it much easie

to get into full business, than in Westminster
Hall. The disputes and controversies of the
neighbourhood were settled in his little bow
parlour; and the effects which he produced
around him, are so well known, that it would
be superfluous for me to give any account of
them. Every thing which attention and kindness could do, was directed to the benefit of
his tenants and neighbours. A regular system
of well arranged benevolence, pervading every
cottage, and reaching every individual around
him, was so successfully administered, and with
such general effect, that few travellers have
ever passed the road through *Monk Appleton*,
without stopping to admire the neatness of the
cottages, the crops of the gardens, the division
of the cow pastures, the beauty of the new
school, the healthy and cheerful looks of the
inhabitants, and the variety of circumstances,
which denoted the industry and happiness of
the possessors —The stone on the Church wall,
which you see from the high road, was put up
by a subscription of the cottagers for several
miles round who each gave the value of *one
day's milk* of their cows. It contains the following inscription.

TO
JAMES GOODENOUGH, ESQ.
THE POOR MAN'S FRIEND,
This Stone
was erected by the Cottagers
of this Neighbourhood.
In Memory
of his Virtues.
and of their Gratitude.

———

He died 28th January, 1808,
Aged 54 Years.

———

Mr. Goodenough had a servant of the name
of JONES, who had had the care of his little
establishment in Chancery-lane. Upon his
coming to the family estate, and removing to
Monk Appleton, he appointed her his housekeeper; trusting her not only with the management of his family, but in a great degree, with
the execution of the plans which he formed for
the benefit of his poor neighbours. He was not
deceived in his confidence: for though she
possessed a liberal mind, and an active and
eager temper, yet Mrs. Jones was frugal and
careful. She held waste to be a deadly sin;
having, with her Master's leave, had painted in

large black letters, over the kitchen chimney, those sacred words, pronounced in the moment of miraculous plenty,—GATHER UP THE FRAGMENTS THAT REMAIN, THAT NOTHING MAY BE LOST. The consequence was, that though his estate was never more than 800*l.* a year, and though he set apart (as other gentlefolks do) a tenth part of his income to charity, yet he lived more respectably and hospitably, than some other Squires, with twice, nay thrice his income, and yet he never run out.

CHAPTER II.

Mrs. Jones determines to visit her Sister—the Journey—arrives at Middle Dean—Family Prayer—View of the Dean.

WHY should I renew my own and my reader's sorrow, by describing the circumstances of the Squire's death, and the unavailing care and attention of his faithful housekeeper? The estate, we all know, went, on his death without issue, to his next brother, Captain Goodenough, then serving in the West Indies. Upon opening the Squire's Will, they found he had left the furniture and stock, and the arrears of rent, to his brother; and the rest of his personal property to his friends and domestics; having given Mrs. Jones an annuity of thirty pounds for her life, with a legacy of one hundred and twenty guineas.—When the concerns were settled, and she found herself her own mistress for the first time in her life, she determined to visit her half-sister, some years younger than herself; who had married, and had a family at *Middle Dean*, in the county palatine of Durham. Her sister had been the wife of John Thomson, a very honest and industrious carpenter. He had lately died, leaving her with five children.

There was something congenial in their situations, which promised mutual comfort. The assistance of a kind sister might do much for a widow, so left, and with such duties. To Mrs. Jones, after the loss of her excellent and adored master, any useful occupation was an advantage.—She travelled down by the coach, stopping at Doncaster for a day's rest and respite; which was more necessary to one, who had lived a settled and quiet life for many years, and had acquired no habits of winter travelling.

The fourth day brought her safe to *Middle Dean;* where, it being darkish, Dame Thomson and her eldest daughter were on the road

side, waiting to meet her, and to shew the way
to their cottage.   The good dame received her
sister with great kindness and affection.   When
she reached the house, the children soon got
the better of their shyness ; and began nestling
around her, asking for one little tale after another, and always liking the last the best.   They
regarded her as a new discovered friend, with
the keenest curiosity, until the desire of rest
made them wish for bed.   Mrs. Jones then said,
" My dear sister, Almighty God has this day
" restored friends and relations who have been
" long, and long separated ; and he has merci-
" fully preserved us during our long separa-
" tion.   Before we go to rest, let us humbly
" bless and praise his name, for all his mercies
" unto us : and I trust we shall find in that tri-
" bute of gratitude, such comfort and consola-
" tion, that we shall never omit it hereafter.—
" I have in my pocket a Treatise on the Sacra-
" ment, by the pious Bishop Wilson.   In the
" 169th page of it is an excellent family prayer,
" which I beg we may all join in, before our
" young friends go to bed.   You must let me
" be your chaplain, while I continue with you."
She then closed their evening with the solemn
and sacred duty of prayer.   Her young friends

retired to their beds: and not long after both
the sisters.

Mrs. Jones arose early the next morning.
She beheld one of those beautiful and brilliant
skies, which seldom enliven the county palatine
in the month of March. She was delighted
with tracing the course of the DEAN, from
whence the village takes its name, down a nar-
row path, skirted with sycamores and birches,
and here and there a larch or straggling thorn,
or mountain ash not yet entirely deprived of
its berries; opening occasional peeps of the
sea for near a mile. Behind her she saw the
detached cottages and houses of *Middle Dean;*
sometimes grouped and connected, so as to
offer the semblance of a respectable town, and
at other times so separated, as to appear a small
straggling village. As she passed, she beheld
the disjointed precipice of a rock, exhibiting
proof of its containing iron. It had remained,
however, undisturbed; for the owner, though,
eager of inquiry on other subjects, was anxious
not to receive information, which might destroy so much picturesque beauty.—She was
proceeding, absorbed in meditation, when on a
sudden she opened on such a majestic view of
the German ocean, with such accompaniments

of wild and beautiful scenery,—that could a
connoisseur have been persuaded to put a fair
value on the landscape, it would have stood at
the price of some thousand pounds.

CHAPTER III.

*Betty Thomson and Her Five Children—Governor
Sancho—A Widow's Consolation.*

WHEN Mrs. Jones got back to her sister's
house, she found they had waited breakfast.—
Dame Thomson was a pleasing and well-look-
ing woman, with a clear and healthy com-
plexion; her age between thirty and forty. She
had five children, two boys, and three girls;
the eldest boy not quite fourteen, and the
youngest child, a girl, about seven. They were
all promising children; wanting nothing, but
that which all other children want, discipline
and instruction. It was their mother's wish,
and she was kind and good hearted, that they
should have all that was best for them; but she
was afraid of attempting much with young
minds, and she was confused and embarrassed
as to every thing that should be done.

As soon as breakfast was over, *my Aunt* (as
they called her) addressed the eldest boy;

" Well John, you are to be stay and prop
" of your family : what do you mean to do ?"

" I should have wished," said the boy, " to
" have followed my father, and to have been a
" carpenter; but that is passed now."

" No ; not passed, my dear boy. You have
" health, and strength, and activity, and (I
" hope) industry, and honest principles ; and
" those are what the world always wants. Will
" you let me be your adviser ?"

" Aye, indeed, aunt, and with great joy."—
" Well then you shall be a carpenter, John ;
" and the best in the neighbourhood."

" And you, my dear James," said she to the
younger boy, " what will you do ?"

" O ! you must tell me, aunt."

" Well, I have a place for you.

" Nay, but aunt, don't you want to draw me
" into a scrape, such as that you told us last
" night, among other pretty stories, of the Spa-
" nish labourer, Sancho Pança ;—who got the
" government of an island for nothing ; and
" after governing it for eight days, and having
" been hard worked, and sadly starved, found
" the island not worth governing, and went
" back contented to his cottage."

" My little fellow, you shall have a better
" place ; you shall be diligent and useful ; and
" then you will enjoy the fruits of *your own*
" *industry ;* and that is better than being sup-
" ported by others ; and so shall Peggy and
" little Sal, and Bet. We will have work
" enough for them all, if they wish it."

" Oh," cried the two little ones, " we shall
" wish it fast enough, if you will stay and live
" with us, and go on telling us pretty stories,
" as you did last night."

The two elder children went to their school ;
and the three youngest played in a piece of
ground, that was called *the garden.* It was a
rood of neglected space behind the house.—
As soon as they were left by themselves, Dame
Thomson entered on the natural and consoling
history of her own afflictions.

" It had pleased God," she said, " to take
" from her an honest and kind-hearted hus-
" band ; but his mercy had blessed her with
" five promising children. She only wished
" she was more capable of bringing them up.
" But you know, sister, I was hardly six years
" old, and you, I believe, were not much
" turned of fourteen, when you went to ser-

" vice. I am afraid my mother was not so
" kind to you as one could have hoped ; and
" yet I do not venture to ask."

" She was not harsh or unkind, indeed, said
" Mrs. Jones. But it very seldom happens
" in life, that the affection of one's own mother
" can ever be supplied by that of another.
" And it was natural I should wish to get my
" bread for myself. I could not be sure that
" I should always have more than an *half in-*
" *terest*, in my father's house."

" Your going, however, (said the younger
" sister) was a great loss to me. It deprived
" me of the blessing of education ; a blessing
" which my poor mother neither possessed,
" nor valued. I might at least have learnt to
" read my bible, and to teach my little children
" their letters, until I can send them to school.
" But, indeed, fifteen shillings a quarter each
" for my two eldest children, is as much as I
" can afford in the *school-way*."

" Nay, my dear sister, is it possible that
" your three little ones cannot read ?"

" Not a word, I assure you."

" But what have their elder brother and
" sister been about ? I am sure they might
" have taught them."

" No ! *but I would not let them*," replied the
prudent Betty Thomson : " *Neighbour Old-*
" *know*, who is the wisest man in the parish,
" tells me, it is *very imprudent* to let young
" people teach one another : they are too young
" to be trusted with education ; and besides, it
" would give them an improper conceit about
" themselves, as if they knew more than
" others."

" So then, for fear of your three little folks
" *learning wrong*,* you have not let them learn
" any thing at all."

" Just so," said she, very seriously.

" Will you then trust me to teach them ?"

" Yes ; for Mr. *Oldknow* says, people are
" old enough to begin teaching when they are
" forty ; and that's about your age, I think."

" Well then," replied Mrs. Jones, " I will
" try."

---

* Dame Thomson was in this a little like Dr. Paley's *pious
and orthodox old lady;* who was so afraid of *thinking wrong,*
that *she determined not to think at all.*

CHAPTER IV.

*A Family School.—Writing in Sand.—A Receipt
for White-washing.*

MRS. JONES found in her trunk two bits of
cards, and on these she printed in a faii hand,
the two first letters. She then procured a
smooth piece of deal board, and got a little dry
sand. Having thus *founded and furnished her
school-house*, she joined her little friends in the
garden; and finding them tired of amusing
themselves, she told them to come into the
little back room, and she would shew them a
new play. " O yes," dear aunt," they all
cried. She then told them, they were to play
at *making letters*, and to try who could make
them the best. She said that she would first
give them the shape of the letters which they
should play at.

She then gave them a card, with the great
letter A drawn out upon it. Her pupils set
to work, and with their little hands successively guided, each filled their part of the sand-
board, with very *rude* representations of the
proposed letter. What, however, was imperfect at first, improved upon trial; and in the

course of half an hour, a handsome and well formed A was made by each of the scholars, with horizontal piles at bottom, and an horizontal tie in the middle of the pyramid.—She then told them that she could not give them another letter before dinner ; but if they would *try what they could do to amuse themselves in the garden awhile,* they should have B to play with in the afternoon.

She kept her promise ; and her three pupils were so delighted with what they had learnt, that they set off to meet their brother and sister on their return from school. Their first question was whether they knew how to make A and B in sand.—" We can read all the " letters, though they be made into words," replied the others.

" That's another thing," said they.—The elder brother and sister, however, on reaching home, and having the means of instruction offered them, supported their rank, and soon shewed that they could draw out the letters neatly and correctly ; and in their play hours, contrived in future to receive the full benefit of their aunt's instructions.

Mrs. Jones's young pupils pressed on so eagerly, that she gave them two letters the

next morning, and two more in the afternoon ;
and in the course of the week they had con-
quered the whole alphabet of great letters.
The small ones puzzled them at first; but the
habit of victory, and the spirit of enterprize
connected with it, enabled them to manage
them in another week, and to call eagerly for
further amusement.

The first Part of the Child's first Book kept
them amused for some time. In the mean-
while, Mrs. Jones, desirous of applying her
first week's fund, had sent to Sunderland, and
purchased three small slates and pencils for a
shilling. Her pupils found that the slate *
was neater and pleasanter than the sand; and

* Mr. Warren, late of Bury St. Edmunds, Suffolk, has invented a new manufactory of slates, containing *engraved
copies for writing and arithmetic*. The scholar may first trace
his letters in the original copy, then imitate them, and afterwards at pleasure erase his own letters, &c. leaving the original engraving in its perfect state. The price is from fourteen to twenty-pence a slate. The pencils are fixed in
common goose or turkey quills, so as to be as near the size
and shape of pens as may be, and to habituate the hand to
the use of a common pen. The Committee has purchased a
parcel of them, which may be had at prime cost, at Mr.
Hatchard's ; though they would rather wish them to be purchased of the ingenious inventor, Mr. Warren, No. 2, Buck-
ingham Street, Strand. The Society of Arts have voted Mr.
Warren a premium of Ten Guineas and a Medal, for his
invention.—11 April, 1809.

in addition to the alphabet, and the printing of two or three words every day from their lesson, they learnt to draw upon the slate the figures for cyphering.

Mrs. Jones had begun her second week; when she took advantage of *market day* (which her sister always attended) to white-wash the whole of the house.—She made her preparation before hand. The only material that was wanting, was a little lime; and she found that half a peck, (which at the rate of sixteen-pence the bushel, would cost her the sum of two-pence,) would be sufficient. But, however, she thought it better to *have it done handsomely, without thinking of expense;* and to white-wash not only the walls, but also the timber and wood-work. She therefore determined to lay out in lime the sum of FOUR-PENCE, adding four-pence more for the loan of a brush and hair sieve, from the man of whom she bought the lime. She had contrived, without her sister's observing it, to get a tub, in which to slack the lime. On this she had poured the water by degrees, and stirred it with a stick, that was broad at one end. When the lime and water were well mixed, and of the consistence of mud, she took it out with a scoop, and strained it through the sieve into another vessel, where it settled to the bottom in a mass of white-wash. After skimming off the little water that remained at the top, she set it by, ready for the work of next day.

The next market happened to be on Lady-day, which was always a holiday at John's school. She therefore told him she had half a day's work for him, for which she would pay him four-pence ; but he must do it well. This he promised ; and as soon as his mother was set off for market, she began mixing her stuff with cold water to the consistence of a thin paint, and the operation of white-washing began ; John being in his old frock, with little James as his attendant, and Mrs. Jones supplying the material, and helping in places where he could not reach. By one o'clock, the work was finished ; and in two hours more the house was cleaned up by the three girls, and the whole was dry ; exhibiting an appearance of purity and cleanliness, which are seldom seen in the most magnificent apartments.

CHAPTER V.

Alarming Expense.—Invective against Finery.—
White-washing a School.—A valuable Present,
—other Advantages.

WHEN Dame Thomson came home she was
alarmed; and said she could never afford to
pay for what was done.

Her sister asked her what she supposed it
had cost.

" Oh," said she, " a great deal too much?"

" Is a *shilling* too much, sister?"

" A shilling? Nay, you are joking."

" No, I am very serious.—The lime cost
" *fourpence*, and the tools and labour *eightpence*
" more. But there is a good deal of the stuff
" left; more than would do such another cot-
" tage."

" Nay, sister, you amaze me. My husband
" and I often talked of white-washing: but we
" thought we could not afford it. How come
" you, then to know so much about white-
" washing?"

" Oh," said Mrs. Jones, " I found an account
" written by one SQUIRE EMM, of Bishop
" Auckland, as to the cost of white-washing

" the workhouse there, which was done under
" his order. It is in this book* here, and
" contains directions all about it. But lime is
" cheaper there, and does not cost a fourth
" part of what it does in your village."

" Nay, that's in our country too, you know;
" what a pity it is the poor should not know
" that TWO PENNY-WORTH OF LIME is enough
" to white wash any of their houses?

" Well, then, shall we ask your neighbour
" Smith, whether she will have her house
" done?"

" Most readily," cried Betty, " and I'll go
" and fetch her."

The widow Smith came in, and stared at all
the *finery*, as she called it; and in return to
Mrs. Jones's offer, said " her house was good
" enough for her; she did not want to hold up
" her head above her neighbours, as some other
" people did; she did not care for that kind of
" *finery*."

" Nay," cried Mrs. Jones, " I must answer
" you, and say that it is *cleanliness*, and not
" *finery*. It promotes health, and it prevents

---

* Mrs. Jones had in her hand the first volume of the
Society's Reports, the directions of which she had followed,
as given in the Report, No. XV.

" vermin. I have plenty of the stuff mixed,
" and at your service, if you will *only accept it*:
" I am not to return the sieve and brush till
" to-morrow evening, so that you may have the
" use of them for nothing : and, as to the work,
" I will shew your eldest boy, how it is to be
" done ; and you know, neighbour, he is older
" and stouter than my nephew John here ; and
" John has done all this house very cleverly
" and nicely indeed." John, who was proud
of his workmanship, came forward to receive
Mrs. Smith's compliments on the occasion ;
and was not a little mortified, to hear her say,
" That her son Timothy was far above any
" such *dirty work.*"

John Thomson looked to his aunt for comfort,—and found it. Her smile restored him to
his own good opinion : and on her suggestion,
he went immediately to Mr. Briggs, his master,
to offer the wash, and his services, *gratis,* in
white-washing the school. The offer was accepted, before John could get through a modest
narrative of what he had done ; or could de-
scribe how gay and spruce the old cottage now
looked. Another holiday was granted to the
boys, for the next day ; and two of the biggest
of them were appointed his apprentices and

assistants. He directed them in the work; observing, that " though they were not very " *gain,* yet they did it as well as could be ex- " pected."

The next morning, John was called forth by the master. " You have completed your job " (said Mr. Briggs) in a workmanlike manner. " I will not offer to pay you for what you have " done without a view to money ; but a worthy " gentleman has just sent me six Bibles, of a " good type, and handsomely bound, to dis- " tribute among the most deserving of the " parishioners. The first of these, John, I pre- " sent to you: and I have written in it the " cause why I have given it. Keep it as a " testimonial of your own good behaviour,— " and as the best book to which you can ever " have recourse,—in prosperity or adversity,— " in pain or pleasure,—and in all the trials and " temptations, to which you may be exposed in " the course of this life."

This, however, was not all. Squire Bird, the gentleman who had presented the Bibles, hearing that John's work was so well done, gave notice in the village, that if any of them wished their houses white-washed by John Thompson, he would pay the expense, being

one shilling each for the lesser cottages, and
two shillings for the larger. John's business
now encreased. He was presented with a sieve
and brush, and was soon able to buy his lime
a great deal cheaper than his aunt had done.
His work was praised; and instead of a little
jobbing carpenter, he is likely to turn out
a *famous plasterer.*

CHAPTER VI.

Job Robson.—-Infectious Fever in the Village.—
Attention of Neighbours.—Water will extin-
guish Fire.

THERE was one *Job Robson,* whose house had
drawn the attention of those who had observed
the improved state of the rest of the village.
It was indeed in a very dirty forlorn condition. But Job was *patient,* and resisted all
offers; saying " it was no use to wash and
" whiten, when the next travellers who took
" up their lodging there, would dirty it as bad
" as ever."—Mrs. Jones's shilling of the next
week and of the week after, were applied in
mending and cleaning her sister's windows;
and in making some little alterations, so that
they would open easily. From that time, with

her sister's leave, the windows were opened,
and the house well aired every day.

As the event happened, this was not done
before it was wanted. One of Job Robson's
guests (a poor woman, travelling to meet her
husband, whose regiment was just landed at
Berwick), was taken sick of the *infectious fever*;
and for want of air, cleanliness, and care, old
Job, and two of his children, had caught the fever
infection. One of them was the little play-fellow of Dame Thomson's youngest girl; and
before she knew she had even got the fever
herself, she had communicated it to her little
friend.

Mrs. Jones found the child was thirsty and
feverish; her eyes heavy, and her countenance
languid. Dame Thomson was at market. The
aunt asked her little niece where she had been;
and was told "she had only been to gone to play
" with Jenny Robson as usual; but she found
" that Jenny had been taken very bad, and had
" been put to bed. Indeed she was very cross
" yesterday. Poor thing, she might well be
" cross; for perhaps, she might feel, as I feel
" now." The careful aunt immediately went
to Robson's house, where she found several
of the village, who had crowded in, to make

friendly inquiries about their sick neighbour. She perceived that they were only just then beginning to fear, that the disorder they laboured under, was the *infectious fever*. Mrs. Jones asked hastily if she could be of any use, or could assist them by her advice. In any event she begged that the windows might be opened, and that they would not press so close about the sick ;—as they not only made them worse, but were very liable to catch the fever themselves. Some vere alarmed at this, and drew back ; but all agreed that the windows must not be opened, as it might give them their death of cold : and as to assistance, the parish doctor was to be there in the course of the next day, or the day after, and he would not be pleased, if any thing was done before he came.

Mrs. Jones returned in haste to her little niece ; and prepared a little mutton broth, which she gave her in small quantities at intervals. Not being able to procure a shower-bath for the child, she got a spunge and some warm water ready. Between five and six in the evening, she perceived a considerable flush in the child's face ; and that the heat of her skin had increased. She then stripped the child,

put her in her own flannel bed gown, and
spunging her with the tepid water, washed her
well all over. The child looked up to her
with delight, while she was doing it ; and being
after that placed in a dry and comfortable bed,
fell asleep almost instantaneously. When the
mother returned from market, she was alarmed
at what had passed ; and especially about the
room where the child slept, being kept so very
cool and airy. But her sleeping child exhibited
such an interesting picture of calmness and
composure, that she thanked her sister for her
good will, and determined in silence to wait
the result.

When the patient waked the next morning,
she was apparently well ; and her mother was
inclined to indulge her wish, and to let her get
up, and rejoin her play-fellows. Mrs. Jones said
that the fever was nearly extinguished ; but,
she feared, not entirely. She gave her niece
some milk and sago for her breakfast, and continued to supply her from time to time with
a little portion of that, or of the broth. There
was a slight return of the fever, and flush in
her face, that evening ; the tepid water was
again applied as before ; and she was replaced
in a comfortable and well aired bed ; sunk into

a quiet repose ; and from thenceforward was entirely free * from fever.

By the time that little Bet Thomson was got well, the parish apothecary had arrived at Job Robson's door. He saw immediately that it was a case of danger, and he appled himself with all the science and skill of the *old school,* to combat that, which would have been speedily and easily overcome, had it been taken in time. He gave directions as to the case of the sufferers, and for preventing the spreading of infection : and promised to be there again early the next day.

Before he arrived, Mrs. Jones had called ; and had put up in the house, a printed sheet, of Dr. HAYGARTH's *Rules* † *to prevent Infectious Fevers.* The parish apothecary, when he arrived, allowed them to remain ; as, he said, *there was some good sense* in them ; and, in any event, they might make people more careful. He found the poor soldier's wife in extreme danger; her fever very high, the tongue furred, her skin dry, and breaking out with spots : herself delirious at intervals, with severe pains

---

* The reader may find several similar cases tb this, in the end of the fifth volume of the Society's Reports.

† See a copy of these Rules in the Reports, vol. ii. App. 2.

in her head and back. She suffered much, poor creature during the day: but in the course of the night, she was relieved by death from further pain.

To shorten a melancholy detail, Robson, and his youngest daughter sunk under the fever; the other child survived; but months and months passed, before she recovered her former health. The care of the doctor, under the divine blessing, prevented the fever spreading further in the village.

CHAPTER VII.

Increase of Confidence.—Vaccination.—Dread of its Effects.

WHILE poor Robson's family was in this state of suffering and danger, Mrs. Thomson began to look at her sister with surprise, and increased affection. She saw clearly the danger from whence her child, and indeed all the family, had been saved by Mrs. Jones's immediate exertions.

" And how comes it, sister, and by what
" art," she said, " that you are as skilful in
" fevers, as you are in teaching and white-
" washing? Is it by true and honest means ?"

" Indeed there is no magic, no black art in
" it. Three other volumes of the Reports which
" I shewed you, and a little experience and
" attention, have furnished all my knowledge
" on this subject. And sister, if folks would
" only consider their own interest, they would
" find in the same book, not only how to pre-
" vent and cure infectious fevers, but also to
" protect themselves and their neighbours
" against what poor folks suffer dreadfully by :
" I mean the small pox,—which has done quite
" as much mischief among the poor, since ino-
" culation has been introduced, as before."

" Well, I am sure, what you mention, may be
" well worth considering now; for they say the
" small pox is in the neighbourhood at present.
" The great Squire has lately thought proper
" to have his two younger children inoculated
" with the small pox. The doctor ordered
" them to be taken out every day for air, and
" the small pox * has by these means got into
" Parkhurst, the little village near the lodge
" gate. It is a sad thing for the poor people
" there: but they say, the Squire has done

* Many similar instances have occurred. See a note to
the Report of the Royal College of Physicians, in the fifth
volume of the Society's Reports.

" nothing, but what he has a right by law to
" do."

" Well, sister, we'll talk of that to-morrow;
" but let us at present think of our little invalid,
" who wants care and nourishing food, though
" I think she will not require any physic."

The success which Mrs. Jones had had in all
she had undertaken, the skill she had shewn,
and the reasons she had given, all produced
effects on her younger sister. This prepared
her (I should observe she had had the small
pox herself) for any thing which Mrs. Jones
might advise. When, however, her visitor
suggested the idea of giving her children the
Cow Pock, in order to secure them against the
small pox, she could not conceal her appre-
hensions. " She had heard," she said " of
" extraordinary diseases, which were the con-
" sequence of such presumption ;—of Chris-
" tians with cow-faces, and horns upon their
" heads,—Heaven bless us,—and the Lord
" knows what ?"

" Did you ever know any of these effects
" produced by the drinking of cows milk, or
" eating of beef."

" Nay, that's a very different thing."

" Different ? but why ? we drink cow's milk,

" and we eat cow's flesh ; and yet we have no
" horns. But let me ask you, after so many
" millions of persons have had the cow pock,
" whether you have ever met with one, who
" had horns, or had the countenance of a cow?"

" No."

" Have you ever heard of such a one ?"

" I cannot say I have."

" Consider, then, my dear sister, when the
" Colleges of Physicians in London, and in
" Dublin, and in Edinburgh, and when all our
" other learned medical corporations recom-
" mend vaccination, and when the two Houses
" of Parliament join in rewarding and honour-
" ing the Discoverer, do you count all that as
" nothing ?

" Nay, it is much, sister."

" But have they any interest in recommend-
" ing the use of it, though they use it them-
" selves? What private advantage can they
" ever have in our applying vaccination as a
" prevention of the small pox ?"

" I cannot suppose they have any."

" Well, then, let us look to the other side.
" Let us then consider the motives of the op-
" posers of vaccination. If a valuable part of
" their business depends *upon their inoculating*

" *for the small pox,* or upon their *curing it* in
" the natural way, *are those gentlemen entirely*
" *without the imputation of interest?* Does not
" their bread depend, in a great degree, upon
" the success of their opposition to vaccination?
" Is it not their business to cry out, like the
" persecutors of St. Paul, GREAT IS DIANA OF
" THE EPHESIANS! Do they not know, that
" *by this craft they have their wealth?* In short,
" my dear sister, will it be wise to receive the
" testimony of a *very few interested persons,* and
" to reject that of the Colleges of Physicians,
" of the Parliament, and of other countries,
" not only in Europe, but throughout the world;
" —who are all uniting in approbation and
" adoption of the benefits of this discovery;—
" a discovery, which has already been diffused
" over the four quarters of the globe; and has
" met with no opposition, except from a *very*
" *few* selfish and interested persons in this
" country?

" In truth, I would not press this so ear-
" nestly, but for the sake of my nephews and
" nieces. By the desire of my dear and ever
" to be revered master, I was instructed in
" VACCINATION. And Dr. Jenner himself,
" twice when he honoured my master with a

" visit, was so kind as to give me some direc-
" tions, together with his book, which I keep
" as a present, separate from my other books,
" and which I shall ever preserve with pecu-
" liar respect. Pursuing his instructions, I
" have inoculated as many as seven hundred
" and fifty-eight persons with the Cow-pock.
" I watched its progress in all of them. I
" trusted to its being a preservative against
" the small pox ; and I have never, in any one
" instance, found myself deceived.—I say all
" this the more earnestly, because I am anxious,
" before this fatal disorder gets too near your
" dwelling, that you may secure your children
" against it. I therefore intreat and beg that
" you will let me write to the proper office in
" Salisbury-square, for some of the vaccine
" matter ;* and give me, my dear, dear sister,
" so far your confidence, as to allow me to use
" it for the benefit of your children."

" You know," replied the other, " you are
" my elder sister : and how much I look up to
" you. It is a hard struggle indeed, for a

* A national Vaccine Establishment has been lately formed.
Any person now wanting vaccine matter, is desired to address
a letter " to the National Vaccine Establishment," under
cover to " the Earl of Liverpool, one of his Majesty's prin-
" cipal Secretaries of State."

" mother ;—and I don't know what *Mr. Old-*
" *know* will say to it:—yet I submit to your
" superior knowledge. You shall have your
" way."

CHAPTER VIII.

Process of Vaccination.—Natural Small Pox.—
How to make a Garden.—Rent and Profit of a
Cow.—Bees.

THE return of the post brought the vaccine
matter. It was applied to the children's arms,
without any reluctance on their part ; such was
their confidence in their dear aunt. The progress of the disorder, if disorder it could be
called, may deserve our attention. On the day
after the vaccine matter had been applied, there
was a very small spot in the part of the arm, to
which she had applied it. Five days after, the
spot became a distinguishable pustule, the skin
around it being a little inflamed, and the appearance that of a pearl upon a rose leaf. On the
ninth day, as to three of the children, (and as to
the other two, on the tenth,) the pustule was of
its full size, about as large as a pea, with a red-
ness around it: on the fifteenth it had changed
to a brownish colour ; and on the nineteenth

nothing remained, except a slight spot in the arm, to mark the security through life, against the poison of the small pox.

Mrs. Jones had made a call upon their neighbour Smith, to offer to vaccinate both her and her children : but she had refused it ; and, I am sorry to add, not in a very civil manner. It was a sad and lamentable thing, however, for her family, that she had been so very obstinate ; for only a few days after, her youngest girl going with a neighbour to church at *Parkhurst,* caught the small pox, from a nurse child,* that was carried near the church door.+ Before it was known what was the matter with her, the little girl had given it to her sister and two brothers, and the mother caught it soon after. Upon this, Mrs. Jones *repeated* her visit, and she now *entreated*, that she might apply the vaccine matter immediately to their arms, as it would *lessen* the violence and danger of the disorder.

* See a note in the Appendix to the fifth volume of the Reports, No. XXV.

+ It is a grievous circumstance, at a time when in many of the capitals of Europe, the SMALL POX has been almost extinguished and annihilated by the remedial means of vaccination, to perceive an increasing mortality by that dangerous and loathsome disease, and to learn from the Bills of Mortality of the preceding year, that 1169 of our fellow subjects have perished by the small pox in this metropolis during the year 1808.

Dame Smith refused; but, however, at the earnest entreaties of Robert, the younger boy, a play-fellow of Jim Thomson, she told him, " if he had a mind to be a fool, he might;"—and he was vaccinated.

As soon as it was known that the widow Smith and her children were *down* with the small-pox, the rest of the village caught the alarm, and avoided coming near the house. Her family would, indeed, have been in a very forlorn and deserted state, but for the aid of her neighbour Thomson's two boys, who carried them their coals and water; and for the assistance which the females gave to the parish nurse. Through the kindness and attention of their nearest neighbours, all of them were saved, except the youngest girl. The younger boy, Robert, had it very gently: but the mother and her two elder children suffered much, and were sadly disfigured. By the last accounts from *Middledean*, we learn that they are still in a very weakly state.

The reader will not be surprised to find that Mrs. Jones acquired every day additional weight with her sister and the neighbours. As the spring advanced, she drew the attention of her young friends to the garden. Her weekly

shilling was for the next month applied in purchasing utensils and seeds for the summer crop.
Every Saturday was occupied by a *new game*
which Mrs. Jones had invented, and in which
she led the way, of *playing at making a garden.*
Their neglected space of ground was soon filled
with every vegetable that could enrich a cottager; and the borders were here and there
adorned by a few flowers. The improvement
soon attracted the notice of Mr. Bird, the
worthy Squire who gave the Bibles; and he
acted in this, as he had done in some other instances; he let Mrs. Thomson have a fine cow
in good milk, with nice keep for her, at two
shillings a week. Mrs. Jones undertook the
management of the dairy, with the assistance of
the two elder daughters, as her hand maids.
Dame Thomson soon found that, besides all the
advantage of the milk, butter, and cheese for
her children, what she carried to market every
week, was worth thrice the weekly rent which
they paid for the cow and her keep; and that
besides this, her two elder daughters were daily
getting more useful instruction, than she could

* See Mr. Kent's Calculations of the Profit of a Cow to a
Cottager, and of the Rent at which a Cow should be let; in
a note to the Reports, No. XVII.

have gained for them, pay as handsomely as
she would.

The early appearance of some of the flowers,
with which she had adorned the front of the
house, and the border of the middle walk in
the garden, reminded her of the advantages
which the *Mongewell* cottagers * had derived
from their bees ; and made her resolve to endeavour to enrich her sister by an addition of
that nature. The swarming time came on,
when she contrived to people, with an industrious race of inhabitants, two new bee-hives ;
which by a little anticipation of her fund, she
had contrived to purchase, and had placed on
a sunny bank in the garden. They appear to
be exercising their honey trade with great industry and success ; and the children are promised that the honey shall not all go to market ;
but half shall be kept, to sweeten their bread
sometimes, instead of butter.

* See an account of a supply of food and employment for
cottager's families, at Mongewell, Reports, No. CV.

CHAPTER IX.

More Employment.—Visit from Mr. Oldknow.—
Tea Party.—Mr. Briggs.—A select and valu-
able Library.—Objections to Novelty.

NEW events have crowded so fast upon me,
that I had really forgot a circumstance, which
was of some importance in the village. Mrs.
Jones being supplied with fresh vaccine matter
from her young patients, offered to vaccinate,
gratis, any of her neighbours, who chose it.
Not only Mr. Briggs, but the Rector, (who was
come down to visit the parish, and to collect
his Easter offerings,) was earnest with his
parishioners, to accept the offer; and they who
had witnessed Mrs. Jones's success in curing
her little niece of the infectious fever, and had
heard of Betty Thomson's children having
assisted their poor neighbour without catching
the small pox, and at a time when they themselves durst not go within a stone's throw of
the door, were all disposed to put some trust in
Mrs. Jones's skill.

Mr. Oldknow had long carried in his face
proof of his having had that disorder, in the
genuine and natural way. He therefore had

no fears of infection ; and made a kind call on poor widow Smith, at the same time inquiring after the Thomsons. When he was told the children had had the Cow-pock, he shook his head, and said, " Neighbour Thomson, I " am sorry you have been so bold ; I must " needs say, more bold than wise. You have " been venturing five fine children here, and " mixing in their blood the disease of a cow, " And I trow you will be very sorry when you " see the horns sprouting from my little godson " Jamie's forehead, and his face grow like that " of a bull calf."

Betty Thomson trembled, and looked at her sister ; who asked the visitor, how the Smiths were that morning. " In very sad case, in. " deed," said Oldknow, " and in great suffer- " ing and danger. There is little hope of any " of them geting better."

" Well James," said she, looking at the little boy, " they say you are to have horns and an " ox's face. But, my love, we won't agree to " that. Come, and let Mr. Oldknow see your " arm."

" Aye, come, Jamie, and let's see what mis- " chief they have done to thee."

Little James shewed his arm, and the spot which he said his aunt had given him.

" What! is that all, my lad? Have ye no " sores and blotches over you? Speak the " truth, my little fellow, and shame the " devil." No, not I, indeed, and indeed, God- " papa."—Come, then, let's feel thy forehead. " Nay, here's no coming of horns that I can " find; and as to face, neighbour, I must say, " I never saw Jamie look so well in all his " life."

" Aye," said the mother, " he looks very " well, and he says he is well; and I hope in " mercy, that things may yet turn out well."

" Well neighbour," says Oldknow, " won- " ders will never cease. I should not now " admire much, if all the learned DOCTOR " BUGG had said about *horns* and *ox-faces*, " should turn out at last to be a *confounded* " *lie*."

Upon his favourable report, two or three of the least prejudiced among the neighbours, brought their children to Mrs. Jones; others seeing how slight the disorder was, and how well they fared in, followed their example; and the few who had been afraid at first, chose

now not to lose their right to the benefit
of it.

Mr. Briggs had been so much pleased with
all he had heard of Mrs. Jones, that he told
her eldest nephew, that if she should be at
home and disengaged the next evening, he
would be glad *to have the honour of taking a cup*
of tea with her and Mrs. Thomson. Mr.
Briggs was a healthy, well looking man of fifty,
rather above the common stature, and of a florid
countenance. His father had enjoyed a small
living in the diocese; and had left him an
orphan, at the age of fifteen years: with a property, which when it was turned into money
produced 850*l.* three per cents. His guardian,
a tradesman at *Stockton upon Tees*, took a great
deal of care of the property, but little of his
ward; who with moderate ability and good
disposition, had nothing better to do, when he
came of age, than to offer himself as the assistant to the superannuated school-master of
Middledean. Not long after, the old man died,
and he succeeded to the appointment. At the
age of twenty-five, he married a young woman
of *Stockton*, to whom he had been long attached.
Her fortune added 350*l.* to his funded property.
Mrs. Briggs lived only two years. She died in

in child bed, leaving a little girl, which very soon followed its mother. Mr. Briggs has since continued a widower.

Such is the history of Mrs. Jones's visitor.— He began with expressing his respect for the skill, which she had displayed in physic; and wished to learn from whom she had received such valuable instructions.

" I know nothing, good Sir, except what I " have derived from a very few books, and " from the little experience, connected with " them.

" Then, Madam, you must have a very ex- " tensive and valuable library."

" No, Sir,—not very.—What I have, (be- " sides my Bible and Prayer Book, Bishop " Wilson on the Sacrament, and another book " presented by a friend whom I respect), are " all in that little box on the window seat."

" Indeed, Madam, I should be curious, with " your leave, to know the contents."

She opened her box and shewed him,

The Pilgrim's Progress,

Law's Serious Call,

Melmoth's Importance of a Religious Life.

The History of Margaret White, Susan Gray, *and Lucy Franklin.*

Robinson Crusoe.

The Cheap Repository Tracts.

The Reports of the Society for the Poor; and
The Account of an Experiment on Education.

" Did you ever see this last book by Dr.
" Bell, Mr. Briggs?

" In truth, not, Madam. I will confess to
" you, that I am no friend to *novelties*. Grand
" schemes like his, may do well for our good
" Lord Bishop: but they don't suit us little
" folks."

" And why not, dear Sir?"

" Because, Madam, the expense of them is
" too great for any but the opulent; such as
" the rich East Indians at Madras, and the
" wealthy inhabitants of the metropolis."

" Nay, good Sir, I cannot agree with you in
" that; for there is far less expense, and far
" less trouble, in the Doctor's new method,
" than in the old one. A worthy namesake
" of yours, established it at KENDAL* with
" great success. For the honour of the family
" name, let it be tried also in your school."

" Were I younger Madam, *to oblige you*, I
" would make the trial myself, with pleasure."

* See the account of the schools at Kendal. Report,
No. XC.

" Will you then let me try it?—Come, let
" me be your usher. Give me two classes of
" your youngest children. Allow me to bring
" my five little teachers with me."

" These little children, Madam, will impede
" you, I fear, more than they can assist you."

" No, indeed, good Sir. Hardly six weeks
" have passed since the three youngest learnt
" their alphabet; and yet you shall see them,
" with their elder brother and sister, take off
" my hands the greatest part of the labour of
" teaching the others. Well, James, and Sal,
" and Bet, will you go and help me?"

" Oh yes, dear aunt," they all cried at once;
and the youngest added, " we'll soon teach
" them how to spell."

" But, Madam," said Mr. Briggs, " are these
" all the books you possess?"

" Good Sir, I hold it far better to have a
" few good books, and to con them well; than
" to read many idly, and carelessly."

" Madam," said he, " I doubt not, but what
" you say may be very true; but I should
" marvel if you found many examples of that
" mode of study, in the great city of London."

" Perhaps not, Sir," replied Mrs. Jones,

" for Reviews and Magazines now make the
" chief part of the study of the metropolis."

" So I have heard, Madam ; but I never
" could believe that the *really* learned could
" collect all the learning, which does them so
" much honour, from Magazines and Reviews."

" And yet, Mr. Briggs, they are sadly slan-
" dered if the fact is not so. I have heard my
" late worthy master, Mr. Goodenough, say,
" that when two of these wise men disputed
" about a new publication, he could generally
" guess what Review each of them took in."

" I wish, Madam, I had known Mr. Good-
" enough." " You would Sir," she answered
with a sigh, " have known a very worthy and
" sensible man."

CHAPTER X.

A new School Mistress.—Donation of Books.—
New method of Teaching.—Cure for Hesitation.

Mr. Briggs had avoided giving any answer
to Mrs. Jones's offer, because he thought it his
duty first to consult the parents on the subject.
About ten days after, he waited on her, and
said that the neighbours in general, and he in
particular (making a low bow) had *so great a*

respect for her, that they were willing *to oblige her*, and to let their children have the benefit of her instruction.

In the meantime she had written to Dr. B., who had been a friend and occasional visitor of her late master. She had heard that he was in town, and preparing to visit the schools then opening at *Bishop's Wearmouth* and *Sunderland,* He replied, that he hoped to be able to call on her in his way to *Wearmouth ;* in the meantime he begged her acceptance of a few books for her school : and though the parcel contained one hundred and thirty-three volumes, she need not be under much obligation to him ; for, being a subscriber to the Society for promoting Christian Knowledge, the books had not cost him quite *a halfpenny apiece,* the whole expense being only five shillings.*

---

* Mrs. Jones was so obliging as to give me a list of the books which I add with the cost of them, marked from the Society's prices.

25 Child's First Book, Part I. - -	0	10½
25 Ditto, - - Part II. - -	0	10¼
24 Ostervald's Abridgement of the Bible, -	0	10
25 Chief Truths of Religion, - -	0	9
12 Sermon on the Mount, - -	0	6
12 Catechism broken into Questions, -	0	9
10 Order of Confirmation, - -	0	5

---

133 Books   5   0

Mrs. Jones, armed with twenty-three copies of the *Child's First Book,** made her first visit to Mr. Briggs's school. The appearance and the countenance of the children perfectly answered to her wishes; and the novelty of what was proposed for them, seemed to engage their attention. She examined her scholars that day; and proceeded the next in the examination of the progress which they had already made. She then divided them into two classes of twenty scholars each, after fixing on James Johnson, the most promising and intelligent of the boys, as assistant to her nephew John, who was the teacher of the first class. She appointed for the other class, Peggy Thomson the Teacher, and her brother James the Assistant Teacher. Her two youngest neices were to be her occasional attendants, and were placed one in the upper and the other in the lower class. She then marked in the Teacher's copy, from the first part of the Child's First Book, a very short lesson of only four words for the lower class; and for the upper class, a lesson not much longer from the second part. Only five

---

* Dr. B. had added from his table, two copies of his friend, the Rev. Mr. Clarke's, Bible Exercises, and two of his own Practical Instructions.

minutes were allowed for the learning of it ;— for the saying of it, ten minutes.—When, however, the lower class came up to say the lesson, the Teacher soon found that they had not *completely* learned it, whatever they had thought. More than *three mistakes* were made; and the class was immediately sent back to relearn the lesson.—The three mistakes were again made, and they were again remanded. They succeeded however, that very morning, in getting, the one class nine, and the other eight lessons, there having never before been an instance of more than two lessons being learnt in that time.

There was in the lower class a good natured boy, one John O'Reilly, who had made two of the three mistakes. This seemed to be caused by his not distinctly knowing the letters. His master had often noticed this defect.—" Lord " Sir," says O'Reilly, " *I know their faces*, as " well as I do yours: but for the life of me, I " never can remember their *names*." Mrs. Jones wished to have this boy.—He had been then a year in this school.—She set him to making his letters, first in sand, and afterwards on the slate ;—and she produced such an effect upon him in three weeks, that he knew not only the

faces, but the *names* of the *four and twenty gentlemen of the alphabet,* and could call them out,
one after another.

The noise that Mrs. Jones's pupils made in
the articulation of their syllables, was, at first,
rather inconvenient to the school. They did,
indeed, vociferate without remorse : and a desire of making themselves heard, a desire which
extends to other houses and assemblies, had
some effect in the increase of the noise. This,
however, did not last long, and they soon returned to a common and familiar tone of voice,
—at the same time, with a considerable advantage ;—that of *distinctly* uttering every syllable,
which they meant to express.

Mr. Briggs had in his school, two very fine
boys of the name of Oxley.—They were brothers. With quick and lively minds, and en-
gaging dispositions, a cloud had been thrown
over all their faculties, by what had been supposed to be *incurable* hesitation. Mrs. Jones
had been particularly anxious, that they should
be in one of her classes. She hoped that by
distinctness of articulation and slowness of
utterance, and by the several syllables being
successively given, something might be done
for them. As soon as she could, she brought

the upper class forward to read by words, as is practised by Dr. Bell: that is of twenty boys standing round, each only reading a single word of the lesson in his turn. The morning in which this practice began, she had taken a little pains to encourage and stimulate them both, and to engage them to prepare for the word, which each knew would come to his turn. The first word happened to be very easy: it was pronounced without difficulty. They succeeded again in the second word; and they afterwards had no difficulty in pro- nouncing single words, as they came to their turn.—This might have been expected; but what took place in the course of a month, could not have been hoped. Mrs. Jones desired me to hear the youngest boy read; and as far as three or four verses, he went on without any marks of impediment. To have tried him fur- ther might have then injured him: but I am mistaken if, a year hence, either of these boys, continuing under Mrs. Jones's care, has any remains of impediment.

The case of another boy, George Greathead, was of a different kind. He had a good un- derstanding, but he was a great calculator; and he had found by repeated experience, that

it was more trouble to learn a lesson, than to
be flogged for not having learnt it ; and that
being punished for not coming to school before
breakfast, was a much less evil than getting
up early. He therefore used to reason with
himself and the other boys in this way ;—
" Can't you see that learning the lesson is worse
" than being whipt ; and that lying in bed is
" a pleasure well worth purchasing with a
" flogging ?" In some of the ancient philoso-
phers he would have found (if he had not been
too idle to look for it) a great deal to support
his opinion. But he wanted not that. He
had made up his mind ; and would have gone
on, and have triumphed in his opinions in spite
of the birch, if Dr. B's system had not put him
in a constant situation of disgrace and shame,
on account of negligence and inattention. He
made his calculations anew ; and he found that
it was much more painful to be always placed
in a state of disgrace and humiliation, than to
take the trouble of learning his lesson. The
result was that he attended regularly, and
learnt his lesson perfectly ; and the probable
consequence is that, instead of turning out an
idle blockhead, he will be a clever and ingenious boy.

CHAPTER XI.

A new Scholar.—Maternal Tenderness.—A de-
sired Visit.—His Majesty's Birth-day.—Grand
Entertainment.—Enormous Expense.

THERE was another little boy in the village,
one Robert Leonard, aged six years, whose
elder brother and sister were in the school.
He was very indignant that so much fun should
be going on, and that there should be so much
to be learnt, and he not there. His father told
him that paying as he did for his elder brother
and sister at the school, he could not pay for
him also : but if the master would take him for
two-pence a week, he might go. The boy was
not deaf; but with full speed set off for the
school, and found the master coming out of
it. He stopt him and said, " Mr. Briggs, if
" you'll teach me well, I'll give you two-pence
" a week."

" I'll teach you well, my nice little boy,"
said Mr. Briggs, " and I won't inquire who
" is to pay for you. You shall be placed in
" one of Mrs. Jones's classes.

" That's all I want," said little Leonard.

Mrs. Jones succeeded so well with her two

classes, that the other children were desirous
of being admitted, into what they considered as
the most pleasant part of the whole school;
and kind parents were induced, not so much
for the improvement, as for the indulgence of
their children, to ask admission into the bottom
of a class, for those who might otherwise have
been at the head of it.

One of the children had unluckily said to
his mother, on coming home, " Mother it
" would frighten you to see our two classes.
" We learn as much in four hours, as we did
" before in a fortnight. We used to get two
" lessons in the forenoon; and those, I must
" own, not very well : and now we dash, whip
" and spur, through fifteen and sixteen lessons
" in a morning; and yet I can't tell how it
" happens, we spell our words better, and un-
" derstand all we learn better, than we ever did
" before." The tender parent was alarmed
for her child; and made the best apologies she
could to Mrs. Jones, for not venturing, *as he
was an only child,* to let him have the benefit
of her instruction.—Her fears, however, have
been since lessened, and at her *only child's* entreaties, she has allowed him to return to what

was become his amusement, though she thought still, there might be some danger in it.

When Dr. B. soon after passed through *Middledean*, in his way to *Wearmouth*, he expressed himself much satisfied with what she had done. The Register Book of Lessons, he said, he was sorry to find, had not been regularly kept. In other respects, the improvement of the children was as much, as could have been expected. On his visit about a month after, he received still more satisfaction ; and (in a manner peculiar to himself), entered into a detail with Mr. Briggs, as to every thing necessary for establishing the new system in any school ; a detail that was not lost on this worthy man.—The new method of instruction, with Mrs. Jones's aid, was in the course of a few weeks adopted as to all the scholars, in a way to be an example to other schools.

Mr. Goodenough had been accustomed, twice a year, to give a feast to his neighbours. That in winter he called the *Festival of Gratitude;* the summer entertainment, was on the 4th of June, and was intitled the *Loyalty Dinner.* After an uninterrupted continuance of near ten years, her heart burnt within her, as the month of June approached. Whatever might be the event at Christmas, she could not bear that the first of these days, after her dear master's death, should pass wholly unnoticed ; and though she wished to be far from any act of presumption, she could not forbear from asking Mr. Briggs's leave, to feast his scholars, on His Majesty's Birth-Day. But she held that every entertainment is more delightful, as it connects itself more with domestic habits. She therefore wished to make a social feast, which might reach all the houses of the pupils.

There were eighty-seven children in the *Middledean* school ; and they belonged to fifty-two families in that and the adjoining parish. Mrs. Jones, on the day before, had purchased two ox's heads for three shillings, and had washed them well and clean. She had added three pecks of potatoes,* some onions, carrots, and savoury herbs, and salt and pepper to the amount of two shillings more ; and she stewed the whole down *very gently;* making up a small fire at night, and renewing it the next

---

* The reader will find this receipt, in Mrs. Shore's account of the manner and expense of making ox's-head-stew, at Norton Hall. Reports, No. X.

morning; adding from time to time as much water, as would supply the waste by boiling.

Great entertainments are not to consist of one dish. She therefore prepared a second. It consisted of the following ingredients ;* twelve pounds of rice, bought by a kind friend at *Sunderland* for four shillings; three pounds of treacle, purchased by the same friend for one shilling, and nine gallons of milk, which being her own, *cost nothing*. These ingredients baked by a friendly baker, produced ninety pounds of good rice pudding; and added a very substantial dish to the bill of fare.

The whole of this was brought into the school room exactly at noon; and the boys and girls, attending with jugs and dishes, received portions which had a relation to their number in family. Each family upon an average received two quarts of soup, with a proportion of meat and fat, and near two pounds of pudding.—The feast, indeed, was costly,

---

* See the account of the benefit of the use of rice at the Foundling. Reports, No. XXV. The reader will probably suspect, as I find Mr. Briggs and some others have done, that the good Dame, who gave this entertainment, is a relation of the *Mrs. Jones*, whose excellent cookery is recorded in the Cheap Repository. I have not been able to trace any connection between their families.

but not extravagant. When Mrs. Jones had
settled all her accounts, she found that she had
entertained one hundred and twenty persons,
at the expense in the whole of TEN SHILLINGS,
—or a penny a head.

CHAPTER XII.

*Village Library.—Lying-in Charity.—Insurance
of Cottagers' Cows.—Parish Workhouse.—
Playing at Gardens—very fashionable.*

THE valuable present of Books, which she had
received from Dr. B., enabled her to open a
Parish Library,* consisting of her own books,
and five copies of those of the Society. Notice
was given in the school room, that if any of the
neighbours wanted books for their children, to
read to them on Sundays, or after work on the
week-days, they might call at Dame Thomson's
after church. Some of them came, and after a
short conversation respecting the discourse
they had just heard from the pulpit, Mrs. Jones
gave them some account of the books which
she possessed. They selected according to

* See the account of Mrs. King's parish library at Steeple
Morden, and that of the Rev. Mr. Wrangham's, at Hun-
manby. Reports, No. LXXXII and CXLI.

their wishes, promising to attend to her injunction, of taking care of them, and keeping them neat and clean, and considering them as her great treasure. Her custom encreased so much in three weeks, that she was obliged to put down her own name and her nephew John's, among the candidates, in order to be sure to keep a book or two at home for their own reading. When I was last at *Middledean*, she shewed me her " Pilgrim's Progress," which in nine weeks had been in nine successive families. It was *certainly not much the better* for its tour ; yet it is very surprising, that it should have been so little soiled or injured.

She has lately begun a little subscription for childbed linen,* which she calculates may be made very complete for three guineas. Half the money is raised, and above half the linen is already made ; Mrs. Jones having employed some poor women in the village to make them, who were out of work. Mr. Bird, who is a great Squire in the neighbourhood, came to visit the school ; when she took an opportunity of shewing him what distress it was to a poor labourer, if he lost his cow ; especially if he

* See the account of the lying-in charities for the poor at Stowe, &c. and at Ware. Reports, No. XXI and CI.

had borrowed money, or run behind hand, to purchase her. She then explained how that had been provided for by a society * in the neighbourhood of *Scarborough*, established for the insurance of cottagers' cows, at the small expense of a halfpenny a month for every twenty shillings insured upon each cow; so that the insurance on a cow valued at 16*l.* would not exceed eight-pence a month, or eight shillings a year. This, she observed, under some regulations, had proved quite sufficient to cover all the demands that could be made upon such a society. He was pleased with the idea, and has promised, on her sending him an account of the plan, to establish a society of that kind in the neighbourhood.

The parish workhouse, it is well known, is a mean building near by the road side. It is in view, just below the church; and though roomy, was last spring rather crowded. Mrs. Jones has had influence enough with Mr. Toms, the overseer, whose son is at the head of her first class, to get two old men, who were not very comfortable there, to be boarded with their own friends, upon an allowance about equal to what they cost in the workhouse. Six girls,

---

* See Reports, No. CXXXIX.

too, who were not old enough to be put out, she persuaded Mr. Toms to place with a baker's widow, one Mrs. *Allum*, who undertakes to teach them needle-work and reading, and to find them board and lodging at something less than their former expense in the house. Mrs. Allum had been called in the village *the wise woman;* because she could read off hand, and sign her own name.

When the new system had gone on for a fortnight, and the classes had been paired off into pupils and teachers, so that every one knew his place, and the whole went on regularly and easily, John Thomson applied to his aunt to ask the master's leave for him and his brother to play at their new game of *making a garden* in the front of the school house. They said they could bring their own tools, and they had saved a few seeds of those Mrs. Jones had bought for them Mr. Briggs was kind enough to allow them to make his ground, in the front of the school, their *play-place;* and to let them admit such of the other boys *to play* with them, as they should select. You may be sure they were very nice in their choice, and we all know that when work is a pleasure, it is sure to be well done. Mr. Bird, the

worthy Squire of the neighbourhood, who
gave the Bibles, rode by once when they were
at play. He was much amused with their
new game; and promised their leader, John
Thomson, that he would send him a large
parcel of seeds ; so that any of the other boys,
who wished *to play at* MAKING A GARDEN at
home, might be supplied. The sport soon
became, like other fashions, universal ; and the
boys played at it for a full month, by the end
of whioh, *Middledean* exhibited a new kind of
scenery. Neat gardens filled with vegetables,
and skirted with flowers,* adorned almost every
cottage in the village ; and there is great reason to hope that the fashion will continue, as
Mr. Bird has expressed an intention of supplying them again with seeds next year, and of
giving premiums + for the neatest and best cul-
tivated gardens.

* Some persons ask what have cottagers' families to do
with flowers ; not being aware that, by a cottagers' garden,
the owner is habituated to pure and innocent amusement, and
his mind is drawn from the alehouse to domestic and intellectual pleasures.

+ See the account of Lord Hardwick's premiums for cottagers' gardens. Reports, No. LXXVII.

CHAPTER XIII.

Expostulation.—A new Bargain.—Last Advices
(27th Oct. 1808,) from Middledean.

In the meantime Midsummer arrived, when it
was to be settled between the two sisters, whether they were to continue their agreement, or
not.   Mrs. Jones asked, whether the terms
on which she boarded, were such as gave
entire satifaction. If they were, she wished
nothing better, than to continue her sister's
guest.

" Indeed, and indeed, my dear sister, I can-
" not go on with them.   I cannot indeed."

" What I pay, then, is not sufficient ?"

" Oh too much, too much ! and in good
" truth you have made a slave of yourself now
" for full three months ; ever since you have
" been in my house.   You have been labour-
" ing all the time, with trouble upon trouble,
" and one work following close upon the heels
" of another."

" When one's mind, dear sister, is set on
" any thing, *labour becomes a pleasure.* But as

" to me I have had no labour. Your children
" have affectionately done for me every thing;
" and whilst I have been teaching them to be
" useful to themselves, I have had the pleasure
" of making them useful and acceptable to us
" and others, and I have recovered my health
" and spirits after a most afflicting event. You
" are my kindest friend and nearest relative;
" and I am most anxious that you should value
" and approve what you have done."

" Oh, sister Jones, believe me I do not want
" gratitude. I feel the value of what you have
" done. You have showered upon me com-
" forts and blessings, ever since you came
" within my door. You have given cleanliness
" and neatness to the inside of my dwelling;
" you have diffused plenty around it. You
" have made my children a blessing to me;
" and my cottage a source of blessing to others.
" You have preserved my youngest child from
" the infection of fever, when she might other-
" wise, like her little friend and play-fellow,.
" have fallen a victim to its poison. You have
" protected her and my other children from
" the ravages of the small-pox; and while you
" have removed from my mind the *film of pre-*

" *judice,* you have made me respected and be-
" beloved in the circle in which I move.—And
" could I *demean* myself so, as to receive an
" allowance, for what in every view is an ad-
" vantage to me?—Continue to benefit us by
" your presence. We are satisfied, and again
" and again overpaid, by the blessings which
" we derive from you."

" Thanks, my dear Elizabeth; thanks to
" you, for your kind and affectionate accep-
" tance of my services. Let me now propose
" another thing.—The worthy gentleman who
" has favoured us with our cow, has at present
" other candidates for his bounty. We need
" not interfere with them. I will purchase
" two cows: your bigging is large enough for
" them in winter; and he has promised me a
" cow pasture, and a hay field, at a farmer's
" rent. That, and the money for the purchase
" of the cows, I will supply; and, with the
" aid of your daughters, I will manage the
" dairy on our joint account. The produce,
" beyond your family consumption you shall
" carry to market. Will you accept my moiety
" of the profits for my board and lodging? I
" beg you will."

" Nay, sister! that would be still more than
" your former allowance. But you shall com-
" mand."

Having been in the neighbourhood of *Middledean*, for near two months this last summer,
I thought it might be useful to give a plain
state of the case, and to shew how much may be
done for the good of oneself and others, *with a
shilling a week*, in the course of three months.
At the same time I should observe, that the
effects of what Mrs. Jones has done, are not
confined to Dame Thomson's house, nor yet to
the parish school, nor even to the village. It
has extended to ALL THE WORLD, FOR FIVE
MILES ROUND : and the progress of *doing better
and better* was not interrupted between Midsummer and Old Michaelmas Day, when I
left that part of the country. By the last letter
from *Bishop's Wearmouth*, dated the 27th of
October, 1808, I find that the eldest boy, John,
is going apprentice, without any fee, to a very
eminent plaisterer at *Durham;* that two or
three respectable families have applied as a
favour, for his sister Peggy Thomson, as a dairy
maid ; and that it is *the talk of all that country,*

that Mr Briggs is paying his addresses to Mrs. Jones :—and more is said,—that it wi l not be for the want of the good offices of her younger sister, if the match does not speedily take place.

7th November, 1808.

INDEX.

INDEX.

INDEX.